Editor-in-Chief and Founder:
  Lyndon H. LaRouche, Jr.
Editorial Board: *Lyndon H. LaRouche, Jr. , Helga Zepp-LaRouche, Robert Ingraham, Tony Papert, Gerald Rose, Dennis Small, Jeffrey Steinberg, William Wertz*
Co-Editors: *Robert Ingraham, Tony Papert*
Managing Editor: *Nancy Spannaus*
Technology: *Marsha Freeman*
Books: *Katherine Notley*
Ebooks: *Richard Burden*
Graphics: *Alan Yue*
Photos: *Stuart Lewis*
Circulation Manager: *Stanley Ezrol*

INTELLIGENCE DIRECTORS
Counterintelligence: *Jeffrey Steinberg, Michele Steinberg*
Economics: *John Hoefle, Marcia Merry Baker, Paul Gallagher*
History: *Anton Chaitkin*
Ibero-America: *Dennis Small*
Russia and Eastern Europe: *Rachel Douglas*
United States: *Debra Freeman*

INTERNATIONAL BUREAUS
Bogotá: *Miriam Redondo*
Berlin: *Rainer Apel*
Copenhagen: *Tom Gillesberg*
Houston: *Harley Schlanger*
Lima: *Sara Madueño*
Melbourne: *Robert Barwick*
Mexico City: *Gerardo Castilleja Chávez*
New Delhi: *Ramtanu Maitra*
Paris: *Christine Bierre*
Stockholm: *Ulf Sandmark*
United Nations, N.Y.C.: *Leni Rubinstein*
Washington, D.C.: *William Jones*
Wiesbaden: *Göran Haglund*

ON THE WEB
e-mail: eirns@larouchepub.com
www.larouchepub.com
www.executiveintelligencereview.com
www.larouchepub.com/eiw
Webmaster: *John Sigerson*
Assistant Webmaster: *George Hollis*
Editor, Arabic-language edition: *Hussein Askary*

EIR (ISSN 0273-6314) *is published weekly (50 issues), by EIR News Service, Inc.,* P.O. Box 17390, Washington, D.C. 20041-0390. *(703) 777-9451*

European Headquarters: E.I.R. GmbH, Postfach Bahnstrasse 9a, D-65205, Wiesbaden, Germany
Tel: 49-611-73650
Homepage: http://www.eirna.com
e-mail: eirna@eirna.com
Director: Georg Neudecker

Montreal, Canada: 514-461-1557

Denmark: EIR - Danmark, Sankt Knuds Vej 11, basement left, DK-1903 Frederiksberg, Denmark. Tel.: +45 35 43 60 40, Fax: +45 35 43 87 57. e-mail: eirdk@hotmail.com.

Mexico City: EIR, Sor Juana Inés de la Cruz 242-2 Col. Agricultura C.P. 11360 Delegación M. Hidalgo, México D.F. Tel. (5525) 5318-2301 eirmexico@gmail.com

Canada Post Publication Sales Agreement #40683579

Postmaster: Send all address changes to *EIR*, P.O. Box 17390, Washington, D.C. 20041-0390.

Signed articles in *EIR* represent the views of the authors, and not necessarily those of the Editorial Board.

Who Was Behind 9/11?

War with Russia, China, and India, or Global Development Partnership?

by Helga Zepp-LaRouche, chairman of the German political party BüSo

April 22—In the absence of adequate public debate on a development that concerns all of our lives and on which the future existence of the human race depends, the world once again finds itself in a Cold War and a global spiraling arms race: The United States' and NATO's attempt to ram through a unipolar world order—although it does not correspond to actual power relations—threatens to set off new wars. In the age of thermonuclear weapons, it would mean the third and final world war.

The simultaneous flare-up of the conflicts in the South China Sea and around the Korean Peninsula, and the situations in the Baltic states and Baltic Sea, in Ukraine, and Southwest Asia are all defined, despite their own specific predicates, by this characteristic: In stark contrast to the official propaganda line which accuses Russia and China of aggressive behavior, it is in reality the United States, Great Britain, and NATO that are working away at encircling and provoking Russia and China.

To this end, President Obama launched last week the Southeast Asia Maritime Security Initiative, funded with $425 million, an initiative intended to forge the seven ASEAN nations, plus Taiwan, into a military bloc against China in the Pacific. In an article titled, "Saving the South China Sea Without Starting World War III," published March 30 in *The National Interest*, the author, Van Jackson, a military analyst from the Center for a New American Security, even urged the creation of an alliance which would bring India, Australia, South Korea, Japan, Indonesia,

MEA India/Vikas Swarup

The foreign ministers of China, Russia, and India met in Moscow on April 19. From left, Wang Yi, Sergey Lavrov, and Sushma Swaraj.

Vietnam, and the Philippines together under U.S. direction.

Chinese international affairs expert Hua Yisheng responded in an uncharacteristically sharp tone in the official Chinese newspaper *People's Daily*, in an article with the headline, "U.S. Fanning the Flames of Potential World War III Will Only Hurt Itself." He described the massive military buildup in the region against China that is already underway, and the picture of Chinese activities there which has been distorted for the sake of propaganda.

Given the obvious orchestration of an escalation of the situation in the South China Sea prior to the ruling on the Philippines' complaint against China before the Permanent Court of Arbitration in the Hague—a ruling expected in late May or early June—Chinese Foreign Minister Wang Yi declared explicitly that, in denying the authority of this court, China is in absolute accordance with Article 298 of the UN Convention on the Law of the Sea (UNCLOS), which excludes any forced settlement and provides instead for solutions to conflict through dialogue and negotiation. The same guideline appears in Article 4 of the Declaration on the Conduct of Parties in the South China Sea (DOC), which has been signed by China and the ASEAN nations. It is rather the Philippines that is aggravating the situation with its one-sided claims.

At the latest meeting of the Russian, Chinese, and Indian foreign ministers in Moscow, Russian Foreign Minister Sergey Lavrov explicitly supported the Chinese position that the conflict should be solved through negotiations between the nations directly affected, and by avoiding its internationalization. At the conclusion of this meeting, in what must have come as a surprise to some, all three foreign ministers signed a communiqué presenting the international treaties which China invokes—UNCLOS and DOC—as the correct basis for resolving the conflict. That makes clear that India has rejected the United States' claim to a unipolar world.

Moreover, the Chinese Foreign Ministry sharply condemned the statement by British Minister of State at the Foreign Office Hugo Swire, that Great Britain fully and totally supports the United States' demand that the decision of the Permanent Court of Arbitration in the Hague be binding on both parties. The only new development, it said, is the more frequent deployment of American airplanes and frigates into the region.

In a similar inversion of the facts, the United States presented the close encounter between the U.S. destroyer USS Donald Cook and a Russian fighter aircraft in the Baltic Sea, as "Russian aggression," although the incident occurred only 70 sea miles from Russian territory, and the Baltic Sea is, like the South China Sea, many thousands of miles from the United States. You only have to convince people that black is white, and white is black, as Bertrand Russell remarked in his time.

Russian Deputy Defense Minister Anatoly Antonov told RT *on April 20 that NATO leaders "are now saying that Russia is 'at the doorstep' of the Alliance, as if it had been Russia expanding its territory toward the Alliance all these years, and not vice versa."*

Obama and His Queen

Meanwhile, nearly 15 years after the attacks of September 11, 2001, there is finally a groundswell for publishing the now famous 28-page chapter of the Joint Congressional Inquiry, which has been kept classified and, according to the then co-leader of this investigation, Senator Bob Graham, shed light on the leading role of Saudi Arabia in this terrorist attack, which changed the world so decisively. This coincided with President Obama's trip to Riyadh, where he assured the Saudi regime and the leaders of the Gulf Cooperation Council that the United States (and NATO?) will defend these states against Iran.

In reality, the purpose is to assert the interests of the British Empire, which persists in the form of the international financial system and the Commonwealth, and which has controlled the manipulated the Near and Middle East since the days of Lawrence of Arabia. Recently Great Britain announced that it intended to again fully impose its interests "east of Suez," in an April 2013 briefing paper by the Royal United Services Institute, described as the leading military think tank of the British Monarchy, entitled "A Return to East of Suez? UK Military Deployment to the Gulf." (An article by Jeff Steinberg, dealing with this in part, is in the June 21, 2013 *EIR*.)

And so, as if there were no commotion over the 28 pages, Obama's trip took him directly from visiting King Salman to Queen Elizabeth—without thought of the Al-Yamamah/BAE agreement of some 25 years ago between the two royal houses, which is suspected of being used to finance terrorist activities. Meanwhile in the United States, pressure is mounting on Obama as to why he continues to maintain the cover-up of the role of Saudi Arabia in the attacks of September 11, the coverup which George W. Bush openly organized.

An insight into this question was afforded in the item Obama published on April 22 in the *Daily Telegraph*, in which he urges the British to vote to remain in the European Union in the upcoming referendum, because they "should be proud" that the EU helps to spread British values across the continent. The Mayor of London, Boris Johnson, immediately accused Obama of hypocrisy, since the United States has never signed on to the International Criminal Court, nor the UNCLOS, nor the UN Convention on the Rights of the Child, nor the UN Convention on the Emancipation of Women. Aside from the public relations version, what are these British values? Wars based on lies that trigger refugee flows to Europe; tax havens and the financing of illegal operations as in the scandal of the Panama Papers now coming to light (or should they be called the London Papers?); laundering of drug money through banks such as HSBC; credit conditionalities that have for decades thrown the so-called Third World into abject poverty crashes—the list goes on and on.

Obama and his Queen.

What Are Germany's Interests?

In light of the escalating confrontation with Russia and China—and thus implicitly also India—it is high time that Germany and other European nations reconsider what their real security interests are. The sanctions against Russia have inflicted significant losses on German industry, and were moreover based on a "narrative" of the Ukraine crisis, which is just as distorted as the story about the alleged Chinese aggression in the South China Sea, or the one about "our allies" Saudi Arabia and Turkey, who still support ISIS or ISIS-allied groups in Syria and Iraq.

Given the immediate strategic situation, and the hair-raising perspective assured us by the current field of presidential candidates in the United States, it is a matter of survival for Germany to rethink its foreign policy. (Hillary Clinton now bears the nickname "Killary." She sees "Russian aggression" everywhere and demands that especially Germany should pay more for the growing military budget of NATO.)

Russia has shown itself to be a reliable and indispensable partner in the case of the negotiations of the P5+1 agreement with Iran and in the military intervention into Syria. China, with its offer of win-win cooperation in the development of a new Silk Road, provides a convincing perspective for a global development partnership. We are on the verge of World War III, and the only chance for America to regain its identity as a republic is for Germany, and therefore Europe, to say no to global confrontation with Russia, China, and India.

This article was written for the German newspaper, Neue Solidarität.

EIR Contents   www.larouchepub.com   Volume 43, Number 18, April 29, 2016

CHOGM/Roderick Cacha

Cover This Week

LaRouche: "Queen Elizabeth was the author of this operation. She was the only person qualified to authorize this operation."

End the 9/11 Coverup

LAROUCHE PAC WEBCAST

Where the Secrets Are Buried

The following is a transcript of the LaRouche PAC Friday Webcast for April 22, 2016.

Matthew Ogden: I would like to welcome all of you to our weekly broadcast here from larouchepac.com. You're watching the Friday evening webcast for April 22, 2016. I'm joined in the studio tonight by Jeffrey Steinberg, from *Executive Intelligence Review*. The two of us had a meeting with both Lyndon and Helga LaRouche, and I think that the presentation that Jeff gives tonight will be a very significant presentation, elaborating on some remarks that Mr. LaRouche made just yesterday on the question of the story *behind* and *beyond* the 28 pages.

As those of you who are watching this broadcast tonight probably know, we are living in a truly momentous period of history. Over the last two weeks, since the "60 Minutes" episode which elaborated the story of the so-called "28 pages," the redacted chapter of the 9/11 Joint Congressional Inquiry report into 9/11, that has been classified by both the Bush *and* Obama administrations—since that broadcast, there has been an unrelenting stream of media coverage of this story, in almost all of the major national press in the United States, and also internationally, in Europe and elsewhere.

There has also been a relentless attack, directly, on Obama, by name, for his refusal to declassify these 28 pages, despite the promises that he has given to the 9/11 families, and also for his open and explicit opposition to the lawsuit that the families have waged against the Kingdom of Saudi Arabia, as well as the bill that they have introduced into the United States Senate, the Justice Against Sponsors of Terrorism Act (JASTA), which

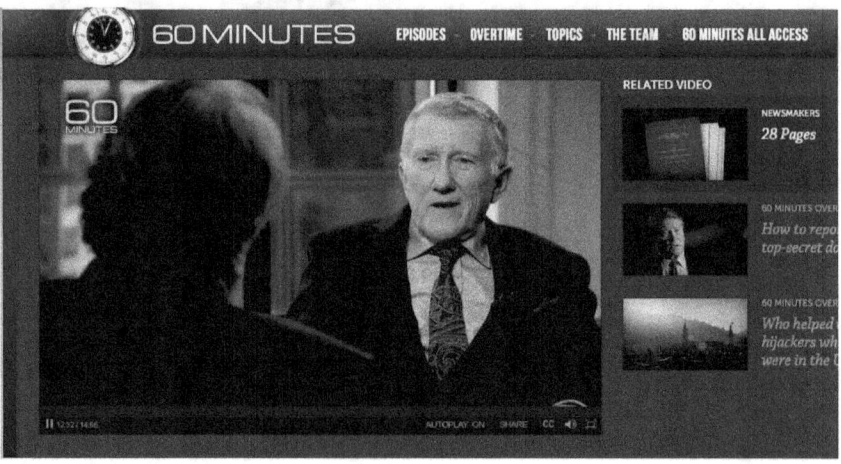

The CBS program "60 Minutes" on April 10, 2016 exposed the story of the suppressed 28 pages of the 9/11 Joint Congressional Inquiry's report. Steve Kroft interviewed former Senator Bob Graham, co-chairman of the Inquiry, and former Secretary of the Navy John Lehman, seen here, a member of the Inquiry, and others.

would allow those victims to sue the state sponsors of the 9/11 attacks.

As you know, on the LaRouche PAC website we have been covering this story for years, very closely. We've been following the efforts of Congressmen Walter Jones (R-N.C.), Stephen Lynch (D-Mass.), and Thomas Massie (R-Ky.) in the House of Representatives, who have introduced a resolution, now over two years ago, House Resolution 14 (H.R.14), which was previously House Resolution 428, calling on Obama to declassify the 28 pages. And they've worked very closely with former Senator Bob Graham (D-Fla.). Graham was the chairman of the Senate Intelligence Committee at the time of the 9/11 attacks, and was co-chairman of the 9/11 Joint Congressional Inquiry report.

Bob Graham has been very vocal, for years, in calling for the 28 pages to be released. I had the pleasure of interviewing him at an event in Florida in November 2014, and at that time, he was very clear that if the 28 pages had not been classified and suppressed, you

Congressman Walter Jones speaks at a press conference on the 28 pages, on Capitol Hill, Sept. 9, 2014, with his colleagues Stephen Lynch and Thomas Massie, and Terry Strada, a leader of the bereaved families, shown here with her children.

would not be seeing the threat of terrorism that we're facing today from Al-Qaeda and from ISIS, both of which have received direct funding from individuals connected with the Saudi regime.

Saudi Threats, FBI Horse Manure

Senator Graham wrote a very clear and *very blunt* op-ed in the Florida newspaper *TCPalm*, titled, "28 Pages: How Our Government Has Used Deceit to Withhold Truth from the American People." This op-ed was published on Wednesday [April 20], to coincide with President Obama's landing in Riyadh to hold a bilateral summit with King Salman of Saudi Arabia. In this op-ed, Senator Graham is perhaps more explicit than he has ever been.

He said, "This was not just a cover-up." The suppression of the 28 pages and other evidence linking the Saudis to 9/11 was the result of what he calls "an aggressive deception." He says, "Your government has purposely used deceit to withhold the truth." The reason for this deceit, he says, "is to protect the Kingdom of Saudi Arabia from its complicity in the murder of 2,977 Americans. On April 15, the *New*

York Times reported: 'Saudi Arabia has told the Obama administration and members of Congress that it will sell off hundreds of billions of dollars' worth of American assets held by the kingdom if Congress passes a bill that would allow the Saudi government to be held responsible for any role in the Sept. 11, 2001, attacks.'" That is obviously a blackmail threat against the United States, and that is what the Saudis said publicly; one can only wonder what they were threatening behind closed doors.

What Senator Graham goes on to say in this op-ed is: "If that is not sufficient to get your blood boiling, read on [the *New York Times* continues]: 'The Obama administration has lobbied Congress to block the bill's passage.'"

Now, Senator Graham elaborates that there have been multiple forms of what he calls this "aggressive deceit"; it's not just the suppression of the 28 pages. He said the 28 pages would disclose the sources of funding for the attack on 9/11; these pages have been under review for declassification for three years, which is three times the amount of time that it took to research, write, and publish the original Congressional Inquiry report, which was 838 pages long! He said, secondly, "The 28 pages are the most iconic, but not the only, evidence to be withheld from the [published] report of the congressional inquiry. The report is pocked by hundreds of specific redactions."

And then he says, thirdly, "Investigations at locales where the hijackers lived and plotted prior to the attacks also have been classified. One of those involves Mo-

Former Senator Bob Graham addresses a press conference in Washington, Jan. 7, 2015, calling for the release of the 28 pages. With him are Congressmen Walter Jones (right) and Stephen Lynch.

hamed Atta, the leader of the hijackers, and two of his henchmen who are alleged to have collaborated with a prominent Saudi family who lived in Sarasota [Fla.] for six years before abruptly departing for Saudi Arabia two weeks before 9/11."

Senator Graham says, "The FBI publicly described its Sarasota investigation as complete, and said it found no connection between the hijackers and the family. Later, responding to a Freedom of Information lawsuit, the FBI released an investigative report that said the family had 'many connections' to individuals tied to the terrorist attacks. *The FBI for two years has aggressively resisted releasing that report,*" Graham says [emphasis added]. And this is part of a much bigger story that goes beyond just the 28 pages.

Now, Senator Graham concludes that op-ed by saying there are three reasons why the 28 pages must be released: One is justice for the families; two is national security, and he said: The fact that Saudis, and their "blatant attempts to avoid liability as co-conspirators in the crime of 9/11, and the U.S. government's acquiescence by refusing to release information (and opposition to reforming laws that would hold collaborators in murder to account) has been a clear signal to the kingdom that it is immune from U.S. sanctions. With that impunity," Senator Graham says, "it continues to finance terrorists and fund mosques and schools used to indoctrinate the next generation of terrorists in intolerance and jihad."

And then finally, he said, this is an issue of democracy. "The American government is founded on the consent of the governed. To give that consent, the people must know what the government is doing in its name. Distrust in government is reflected in the speeches of today's presidential candidates," he said. "The public's sometimes angry response is fueled by a sense of betrayal and deceit."

It's the British Monarchy

Mr. LaRouche was asked a relevant question from an institutional source this week, which reads: "Mr. LaRouche, there has been an overwhelming enthusiasm to release the 28 pages lately. What is your advice to the Obama administration, in regard to the 28 pages?"

We produced a short video which includes the audio

White House/Eric Draper

President George W. Bush meets with Saudi ambassador Prince Bandar bin Sultan at the Bush ranch in Crawford, Texas, Aug. 27, 2002.

of Mr. LaRouche's remarks on this subject. We're going to play it for you now, and then I'm going to ask Jeff Steinberg to come to the podium to elaborate some of the points that Mr. LaRouche asserts in this statement.

Lyndon LaRouche: [recorded voice] I was watching those two planes which were carrying the victims, and carried them to death. I was an eyewitness to the press. We knew that they were being carried, as victims, inside the planes, in the two planes in succession, and obviously the passengers all died.

But that operation, on that occasion, which I witnessed from beginning to end, defines the actual issue which has to be addressed.

Now of course, I also knew what the background was. The way this thing was set into motion was with the *Bush family*. The Bush family was actually a key part of setting this thing into motion; they may not have intended to do that, because they're too stupid to know what they're doing. See, the Bush family was involved in its own little warfare operation, so there was a spillover from the Bush administration as such, into this particular operation. The whole operation was twofold: One, was British-Saudi operation. Now the person who was directing the thing from inside the United States, had been trained by the British system. Bandar was a key figure operating inside the United States. Bandar was directly overseeing the launching of this operation.

And they were shipping petroleum as a real money-

Creative Commons/Roberta Bocchese

LaRouche: Her Majesty the Queen was the author of the 9/11 attacks, the deliberate murder of American citizens. Here, Queen Elizabeth and Prince Philip in 2011.

making operation, just with the oil trade, by the British, shared with the Saudis; and this thing was done for harmful purposes in many ways, and was a key part of control of what the United States was doing in petroleum; because the thing was a fraud—a fraud committed by Her Majesty. Her Majesty was guilty, period. Queen Elizabeth was the author of this operation. She was the only person who was qualified to authorize this operation.

The attack on Manhattan was done under the cover of the *British system*. And the Saudis were a subordinate aspect of the British system as a whole. Her Majesty was the author of this monster. And the Saudis were simply stooges. The Saudis have been stooges from the beginning of the 20th century. That's the essential story. Everything has to be focussed on that: The fact that is was the *deliberate mass murder of American citizens*. And not only that, but a *direct attack* on the United States!

The key thing is that the British and the Saudis are the same thing, since that time. And all these facts are really known, on the record. The Saudis are guilty and the British are guilty, because the Saudis and the British are part of the *same agency*. What the Saudis do, what the British do, *won't* be the same thing. The fact is that the Saudi Kingdom is not a real government—it's an empire; it's an imperial institution. It has no formal responsibility to anything except the Kingdom of the Saudis, and the British! They *are* the same thing!

Ogden: Now, as you can see displayed on the screen, we have a short advertisement for a much longer feature documentary that was published several years back by LaRouche PAC Television, which was called, *Beyond the 28 Pages: 9/11 Ten Years Later*. It is also available here on the LaRouche PAC YouTube channel.

Jeffrey Steinberg was interviewed as part of that production, and obviously he has been very intimately familiar with many of the facts that are presented in that documentary and which were alluded to by Mr. LaRouche in the statement that you just heard. So I'm going to invite Jeff Steinberg to come to the podium to elaborate this, in a little bit more detail.

Britain Created Saudi Arabia

Jeffrey Steinberg: Thank you, Matt. I think it's important to recognize that the fundamental point that Mr. LaRouche just made in answering the institutional question, is that the story of 9/11 is incomplete if we simply stop with the now obvious, transparently evident role that high-ranking figures within the Saudi royal family and within the Saudi government played in the 9/11 attacks—before the attacks, as the attacks were happening, and in the cover-up that followed. What's crucial to understand is that the Saudis do *nothing* without full support and approval coming from the highest levels of the British monarchy, all the way up to the Queen herself and to the Royal Consort, Prince Philip.

Going back centuries, back to the time of the heyday of the British East India Company, the entire Persian Gulf region was a British colony, a British protectorate. For centuries, every one of the so-called nations—really tribal collections—along the Persian Gulf, whether it was Bahrain, or the UAE, or Qatar, or Oman, or Saudi Arabia, or Kuwait,— all of those countries existed in name only. All of them had treaty agreements by which their foreign and defense policy was run out of London. It was a vital feature for the functioning of the British East India Company to have a way station en route to India and on to China. So, at the beginning of the 20th Century, individuals like Lawrence of Arabia forged the establishment of the House of Saud as a marriage between a tribal family and the Wahhabi fundamentalist clergy of that area: It's always been a British game, it's always been tightly under the thumb of the British. And that carries through even more so in the present modern period.

Mr. LaRouche mentioned Prince Bandar bin Sultan, who for years was the Saudi ambassador here in the United States; before that, he was the Saudi military attaché in Washington. And he was widely referred to as "Prince Bandar Bush" because of his close relationship with the Bush family, starting with father George H.W. Bush. And he was notoriously close to George W. Bush. But above all else, Prince Bandar was a British agent. He was trained at British military schools; his official, authorized biography was written by one of his school chums from British military school. And in 1985, Bandar negotiated what came to be a critical feature of the Anglo-Saudi arrangement—the Al-Yamamah deal; this was ostensibly a barter arrangement by which the Saudis paid in oil for British military equipment—fighter planes, radar systems, training, supplies, all of that.

Public domain/St.J. Philby, The Heart of Arabia, 1922

British agents such as St. John Philby (shown here in Riyadh) and T.E. Lawrence ("Lawrence of Arabia") studied the Wahhabi perversion of Islam and arranged the establishment of the House of Saud as a marriage between this tribal family and the Wahhabi clergy. Philby operated under "anti-British" cover.

Al-Yamamah Funds Dirty British Ops

And in carefully investigating that program, we discovered that the amount of oil that the Saudis delivered to the British in payment for about $40 billion of military hardware, was worth much more than that by orders of magnitude. For the Saudis, the oil was cheap; it cost less than $5 a barrel to pull it out of the ground and load it onto a supertanker. But once British Petroleum and Royal Dutch Shell took control over that oil, they sold it on the spot market at phenomenal mark-ups.

From 1985 until the scandal first broke in 2007, more than $100 billion in excess funds were accrued after paying for the British military equipment and after generous bribes to many British and Saudi officials. Hundreds of billions of dollars were sequestered in offshore bank accounts, and those funds represented the

biggest slush fund in the world for carrying out destabilizations of governments, terrorist activities, and assassinations.

Prince Bandar, not being the brightest guy on the planet, openly boasted about this special relationship, and said that while Al-Yamamah was a traditional barter arrangement—oil for weapons—it was in fact something much more. It was a reflection of the "marriage" of the British and Saudi monarchies and of the ability of these monarchies to operate outside of any parliamentary or Congressional scrutiny—and to carry out black operations anywhere in the world that they chose.

Officially, Prince Bandar received a $2 billion commission for arranging the Al-Yamamah deal. And those funds have been traced. They went from accounts of the Bank of England, accounts from the British Ministry of Defense that oversaw the Al-Yamamah arrangement, and went from there into bank accounts in Riggs National Bank in Washington, D.C., the private accounts of Prince Bandar bin Sultan. In the documentation contained in the 28 pages that Presidents Bush and Obama have kept from the American people, is evidence, paper trails, of funds that were sent directly from Bandar's and his wife's personal bank account into the hands of two Saudi intelligence agents who were the handlers of the original two 9/11 hijackers who arrived in the United States at the beginning of the year 2000.

So, the British hand in 9/11 is unmistakable. If those 28 pages were to be opened up, it would not only confirm that the British and the Saudi royal families were together engaged in setting up and financing the 9/11 attacks: It would open up an array of other questions about follow-on terrorist operations on a global scale. All told, hundreds of billions of dollars laundered offshore—probably in places like Panama, as well as the Cayman Islands, the Isles of Jersey off the coast of England—have gone into countless operations

Saudi Press Agency

Prince Bandar is the British agent who worked out the Al-Yamamah deal with his British masters in 1985. Here, Bandar welcomes Tony Blair to Jeddah in 2007.

like the 9/11 attacks themselves.

While many people are quite clear on why it is that President George W. Bush would order the suppression of the 28 pages, because of his notoriously close relationship with Prince Bandar and the Saudis, many people scratch their heads and say, "Well, why would President Obama—particularly after he promised the families that he would declassify the 28 pages—why would Obama continue the cover-up?"

It's not for Obama a matter of the Saudis; for Obama it goes to the next higher level in this whole story, namely, the British. Obama, from the beginning of his political career, has been sponsored by the British. It's not surprising that this week President Obama made a trip to Saudi Arabia; he was there Wednesday and Thursday. He met with King Salman of Saudi Arabia and on Thursday, he met with all of the leaders of the Gulf Cooperation Council countries. From there he has now flown on to London, where he will be holding a private audience with the Queen. Obama has been a slavish loyalist of the British Empire, of the British monarchy, since the moment he came into office as President. So Obama's hand in the cover-up, the shameless continuing cover-up of what happened on 9/11, is all about protecting the British side of this story. Were those 28 pages to be opened up, the minute that one began looking at the role of Prince Bandar, it would become absolutely obvious that there is a major British side to this story.

Now of course, when you talk about the British monarchy, if you roll the clock back just a few years before the September 11, 2001 attacks, you will re-member that there was an intensive investigation over a number of years into the fact that the British monarchy was unquestionably behind the murder of Princess Diana. It was a revenge killing because she represented forces that were completely disgusted with the way that the House of Windsor—Queen Elizabeth, Prince Philip, Prince Charles—operated. So you have a British monarchy that has blood on its hands going back a very long time, and most recently with the top-down ordered assassination of Princess Diana. It should come as no surprise that that same British apparatus is up to its eyeballs in global terrorism.

Britain a State Sponsor of Terrorism

Now in point of fact, in early 2000, *Executive Intelligence Review* filed a formal request with the U.S. State Department that it consider placing Great Britain on the list of state sponsors of terrorism. People may remember that at that time, there was a wave of terrorism going on around the globe. In 1997, the Egyptian Islamic Jihad group carried out an attack against a group of Japanese tourists at Luxor, and the Egyptian government at that time provided detailed evidence that the terror plot had been organized, financed, and controlled by Egyptian terrorist networks that were living in Britain under the protection of the British monarchy.

Several years later, the Russian government filed a series of formal diplomatic demarches because they had evidence that the British government was facilitating the recruitment of Chechen terrorists who were allowed to travel to Afghanistan from Britain to be trained by Al-Qaeda and then safely routed into Chechnya to become part of the separatist terrorist networks that were fighting against the Russian government. There was detailed evidence that was included in that *EIR* profile, and unfortunately, needless to say, the State Department sat on it, did nothing; and so we had 2001. And we had many subsequent terrorist events that followed from that.

So the bottom line here is that, now that there is intensive momentum demanding the declassification of those 28 pages, what is really required is a complete, *de novo*, top-down investigation into the 9/11 actions and into all of the subsequent terrorist actions that have followed and have been the work of the same Anglo-Saudi apparatus. Once those 28 pages are made public, once the American people—led by the families of those 2,997 people killed in the 9/11 attacks—have the chance to thoroughly read through and digest the content of those pages, then the

LAROUCHE
IN 2004
www.larouchein2004.com

Lyndon LaRouche Warns: Jacobin Terror Aims at D.C.

The following statement was issued by 2004 Democratic Party Presidential pre-candidate Lyndon LaRouche on Aug. 24.

All reports from reliable sources indicate that the international terrorist movement which surfaced at Seattle, mobilized itself at Porto Alegre, Brazil, and created bloody violence at Genoa, is now taking aim at the U.S. national capital, Washington, D.C. It is extremely important that those elements of U.S. organized labor who have permitted their organizations to be entangled in sympathy for this terrorist gang, break openly from the operations already being prepared for the terrorist-style riots now being prepared for both the District of Columbia and areas of the adjoining states.

Two leading points are to be made about that present new wave of international terrorism

First, the hard core of the organizers of the present terrorist operations represents the fourth generation of a series which began its existence as an organized international movement of terrorism, during the middle to late 1960s, the anti-nuclear terrorist rampage of the late 1970s, and the terrorist wave of the mid 1980s. As typified by the case of Tony Negri, and the role of the Basque terrorist organization ETA, there is no break in the continuity of the hard-core leadership of these terrorist forces over the period from its exploitation of the anti-Vietnam War setting of the late 1960s, to the present day.

A TERRORIST ON THE RAMPAGE in Genoa at the Group of 7 meeting in late July

ostensibly confident that since they were tools of the Duke, he would arrange for their secure passage. To silence the tongues of those guards, the mob removed the guards'

ism, are standard practices for "warfare conducted by other means."

This was the case of the terrorist facets of the civil disturbances of the 1960s, 1970s

of not fighting for positive solutions, rather than purely negative protest against some isolated aspect of the total situation to be faced.

As I have taught on all relevant occasions, whether in physical science, in economics, or in personal life, the word "principle" should never be used to express anything but the equivalent of a universal physical principle. The only thing really worth fighting for, is the outcome of your having lived, your nation having existed in your lifetime. What is important is what we transmit to become the reality of the generations yet unborn. In what we do to that effect, lies our true personal identity, our only fundamental issue of universal principle.

The most depraved of all "single-issue" politics and other tactics, is the brainless practice of making an alliance with the Devil himself, if the Devil is doing something unpleasant to someone we have identified as an enemy of the moment.

I pick on trade unionists, only to illustrate the same point which could be made for many other parts of society.

Some trade-unionists rationalize their toleration of the terrorists because of an argument which runs more or less as follows: **1)** NAFTA and other forms of globalization are robbing American working people of their jobs and income. **2)** The terrorists who surfaced at Seattle, Teddy Goldsmith's Porto Alegre conference, and the Genoa riots, "say they are fighting against globalization." **3)** Those terrorists are part of a very big and

---

On Sept. 11, 2001, the LaRouche movement was distributing this statement issued by Lyndon LaRouche on Aug. 24, anticipating British-sponsored terrorism in Washington in the immediate days ahead.

---

whole can of worms, the whole British-Saudi empire structure has to be brought down. It has to be subject to the kind of rigorous criminal prosecution that is warranted, and that also means that both President Bush and President Obama have to answer for their criminal roles in both facilitating and covering it up.

As Mr. LaRouche said in his brief comments to colleagues yesterday that you just saw in that 5-minute video, he was on the scene; he was giving a live interview to Utah radio broadcaster Jack Stockwell. He had the TV on in his study, and he saw the planes crashing into the two World Trade Center towers in real time. He was one of the few people on Earth—perhaps the only person outside of those who committed the crime—who understood the full strategic implications the moment that the attack occurred.

LaRouche had warned at the beginning of 2001, once he saw the character of the Bush/Cheney administration, that this was the kind of regime that would look for the first opportunity to carry out a Reichstag fire in order to go for dictatorship. And he understood that it was the Anglo-Saudi apparatus that represented the capability for carrying out just such a heinous crime with those particular intentions. He made very clear in that real-time interview with Jack Stockwell that the entire blame was going to immediately be placed on Al-Qaeda, but he said that, to the extent that al-Qaeda had anything to do with it, it was a bit part. It was a minor element of something much bigger that goes much

higher and goes up to the British-Saudi apparatus that we have been discussing here.

Members of Congress who have read those 28 pages—and by now, well over 100 members have done so—they've all come away with the same conclusion. That these documents must be made public, and furthermore, that they completely alter how you understand the history of the last several decades. So take that as just a glimmer of an indication of what the implications are. Regardless of what's contained in the 28 pages *per se*, it's the implications of the findings in those 28 pages that is important and the can of worms that is opened up that leads all the way up to the British monarchy. And you must realize that the fight to get these 28 pages released to the public is a fight for the very survival of mankind going forward from this day. The British Empire today is bankrupt; it is desperate.

The Empire's leadership is not just desperate to cover up the 28 pages and the whole 9/11 story and the Al-Yamamah story; it is desperate because it's on the edge of losing its power. And it *will*—if the opportunity presents itself—create the conditions using these kinds of capabilities, for starting a world war. So the stakes are enormous, and the answer is very straightforward. Release the 28 pages, and on that basis re-open from the top down a complete and thorough investigation. Start with the British and Saudi monarchies and work down from there. We owe it to the families that suffered through 9/11; we owe it to the American people; and we owe it to mankind.

Ogden: Thank you very much, Jeff. Some of these connections are not unknown to people who are familiar with this investigation. In fact, Senator Graham himself, while denied from including them in his non-fiction book, *Intelligence Matters*, includes some of them in his work of fiction, *Keys to the Kingdom*, which he said he had to publish, because it was the only way he could get the truth into written form. In this novel he includes a lot of references to exactly the kinds of things that Jeff just went through. The role of BAE, the Al-Yamamah deal, the offshore tax havens, the Cayman Islands, the fact that Tony Blair intervened to shut down the investigation into the connection between the British BAE Systems and the Saudis. So, in fact, these are the lines of inquiry that anybody who is serious—and the people who are familiar with this case—wish would be pursued, because they know exactly how big this can of worms really is.

The Declassified 47 Pages

Now, the 28 pages may not have been declassified yet, but there is one very important document that *was* declassified recently, and has only now begun to receive media attention, starting with an exclusive report and analysis by Brian McGlinchey, the editor of the very important website, 28pages.org. This is a 47-page draft document written by two researchers who were working for the 9/11 Commission, the official, independent blue-ribbon panel authorized by Congress and the President to investigate 9/11.

These two researchers, Dana Lesemann and Michael Jacobson, had both been formerly employed by the Joint Congressional Inquiry. And in this 47-page document, they lay out their plans for follow-up research along the specific lines which they had been engaged in while working for the Congressional investigation. One of the items which they cite in this document—and Jeff will elaborate on this—is that an alleged Al-Qaeda operative, a person named Ghassan al-Sharbi, who had trained for flight lessons in Arizona prior to 9/11, and who was subsequently captured in Pakistan, was discovered to have buried a cache of documents near the location where he was hiding, which included his U.S. pilot certificate, which was in an envelope from the Saudi embassy in Washington, D.C.

Senator Graham, who was not informed of this discovery at the time, but learned of it after this declassification, said in response, "That's very interesting. That's a very intriguing and close connection to the Saudi embassy." The second item which is of extraordinary interest in this 47-page research document, are the two questions which these two researchers intended to pursue. The first question was: How aggressively has the U.S. government investigated possible ties between the Saudi government and/or royal family and the September 11 attacks? And number two: To what extent have the U.S. government's efforts to investigate possible links between the Saudi government and/or royal family and the September 11 attacks been affected by political, economic, or other considerations?

Now, what's very telling is that when Dana Lesemann attempted to go back and access the 28 pages which she herself was instrumental in researching and writing, first she was denied access to them, and then when she circumvented that denial, she was fired. She was dismissed from the 9/11 Commission investigation. So I think that just demonstrates in a very illustrative way just one example of what Bob Graham described as the "aggressive deception" that has been undertaken in this case; that's what he said in the op-ed which I cited at the beginning of this broadcast tonight. He said, "Your government has purposely used deceit to withhold the truth." And that is not the only case.

I would like Jeff to elaborate on the entire story of the Sarasota cell and the very significant work that investigative journalist Dan Christensen has done at the *Florida Bulldog*, in tracking down 80,000 pages of FBI documents that linked Mohammed Atta and other members of the Sarasota cell to people connected with the Saudi royal family and the Saudi government. These are documents which the FBI withheld from Bob Graham at the time of the Congressional investigation; they did not tell him the documents existed. They impeded that investigation and stonewalled until an FOIA lawsuit forced them to at least hand them over to a judge. The review of those documents still has not been completed.

So, I would like to ask Jeff to come to the podium and elaborate on the further implications of this "aggressive deception"—not just a cover-up—that has been committed by the U.S. government in this regard.

Steinberg: The 28 pages are a critical piece of this story, because that was the final product; It was the work product after a year of investigation by the Joint Congressional Inquiry. And that 28-page chapter that took up the question of foreign support and funding for the 9/11 hijackers, represented the most solid and corroborated evidence that the investigators were able to compile in the face of massive obstruction.

It's not simply that President Bush, when he reviewed the final 800-page report of the Joint Congressional Inquiry, simply ordered the suppression of the 28-page chapter. Every step along the way, during both the period of the investigation by the Joint Congressional Inquiry and the later 9/11 Commission, was impeded top down from the White House, and particularly from the highest levels of the FBI. This is not mere speculation. In the recent period—just over the course of the last year—many of the documents that were work-products of the Joint Congressional Inquiry and the 9/11 Commission which were classified, have now been reviewed and declassified.

Top-Down FBI Obstruction

For those who don't know some of the inner workings of Washington, there is a board located at the National Archive called the Interagency Security Clearance Appeals Panel—referred to as ISCAP. It is the final authority; it is a kind of Supreme Court with respect to questions about what documents should be declassified. It has been in the process of reviewing and declassifying some of the important staff documents of the two investigative bodies.

Last July it declassified about 29 documents that were work-products from the 9/11 Commission, and one in particular, written by Dana Lesemann and Michael Jacobson, is very revealing. It was a work-product document; it was classified as "Secret," but what they laid out were their plans for pursuing the investigation over the next several months. It is very clear that they had many, many more leads on many more officials of the Saudi government—in southern California, in Washington, in Saudi Arabia—who were deeply implicated with the 9/11 hijackers. One section of Document 17, the name of this 47-page paper that was declassified last July, is headlined "A Brief Overview of Possible Saudi Government Connections to the September 11 Attacks"; it goes through the names of 18 Saudi officials who were in southern California, in Washington, and in Saudi Arabia, who had direct contact with, and facilitated the efforts of the hijackers.

The FBI was a continuous obstacle from the top down. During the "60 Minutes" broadcast several weeks ago, Commission Member John Lehman said that the order to block the publication of the 28 pages came directly from Robert Mueller, who was the director of the FBI at the time. Now, it so happens—and again it's repeated throughout this 47-page working document from the 9/11 Commission staff—that the two 9/11 hijackers, al-Hazmi and al-Midhar, who were living in the San Diego area, were living for the better part of a year in the home of a man who was an FBI informant, who was being paid $3,000 a month by the FBI to keep tabs on possible radicals inside the Muslim community—particularly the Saudi Muslim community in the southern California area.

The staff of the 9/11 Commission, and earlier the staff of the Joint Congressional Inquiry, repeatedly asked to interview the informant; they were blocked at every turn. The informant was put in the Federal Witness Protection Program under a change of identity; the FBI Special Agents who were the handlers of this informant were also blocked from being interviewed. In other words, the FBI, an arm of the Executive Branch of the Federal government, was working overtime to prevent the investigation from going forward.

Going all the way back to the days of J. Edgar Hoover, it was notorious that the FBI was completely in bed with the British. During World War II, it was an open collaboration between the FBI and the British Special Operations Executive headquartered at Rockefeller Center in New York City. But this relationship continued. Wall Street is an important intermediary between the FBI and the British. And so the FBI role in the cover-up, both in San Diego and in other parts of the country, is absolutely stunning; and is something that in and of itself must be thoroughly investigated and exposed.

In the case of Sarasota, the FBI conducted an exhaustive investigation of a wealthy Saudi family that was intimately tied through business with the Saudi royals, and that was in regular contact with Mohammed Atta and two other 9/11 hijackers. The family lived in a gated community in the Sarasota, Florida area. Mohammed Atta and the others would frequently visit that home. Then two weeks before the 9/11 attacks, the family picked up and left the country on very short notice. First they flew to London, and from London on to Saudi Arabia. The FBI compiled 86,000 pages of documentation in following up those leads, because the connections between this leading Saudi family and the 9/11 hijackers was unmistakable. Those documents were withheld from the Joint Congressional Inquiry, despite the fact that the FBI was subpoenaed all over the country to turn over any records relevant to the investigation into 9/11.

FBI Protects British-Saudi Alliance

So you've got "willful deception"—as Senator Graham said—at the highest levels of government. Now we know about San Diego, and we know about Sarasota. We know also that Herndon and Falls Church, Virginia constituted another center of activity of some of the hijackers and some of the leading Saudi clerics who were part of the overall structure of support for those 9/11 terrorists. Paterson, New Jersey was another such center. Senator Graham has said at press conferences on Capitol Hill that we've barely scratched the surface, because the government—to protect the British and the Saudis—has put up a wall of deception. It has blocked lines of inquiry; it has concealed documents; it has committed fraud and perjury. All because the power of the British and of the British/Saudi alliance is so dominant over politics in Washington that the FBI, in effect, is sworn to defend that relationship, even if it means that the American people are denied justice.

So once again, in conclusion, there is much more to this story than merely the events of September 11, 2001, as horrific and dramatic as they were. The 9/11 families deserve nothing less than the full and complete truth, no matter where it leads. But the problem runs much deeper. What happens if we don't purge this Anglo-Saudi problem, if we don't get to some of the questions that were posed by the 9/11 Commission staffers? Questions such as "Did the FBI intentionally withhold from the Joint Inquiry, information about the informant's relationship with the hijackers, and did it subsequently attempt to obstruct the Joint Inquiry's investigation of the matter? If the FBI did withhold information and obstruct the Joint Inquiry's investigation, were the FBI's actions indicative of a larger pattern of FBI non-compliance with Congressional oversight? And what should be done about it?"

This is a can of worms that must be opened and must be systematically investigated, because our very future may depend on getting to the bottom of it.

Ogden: And we are seeing a truly momentous shift around this while Obama is in Riyadh and then flying directly to London. This has become the subject of coverage in almost all media in the United States. And it's an extraordinary opportunity to pull this thread to unravel this empire. However, this is just one of many threads that can and must be pulled.

There are other threads, such as what came out two years ago in the Senator Levin report on the Hongkong Shanghai Banking Corporation (HSBC). This has a major aspect to it, and of course, this is becoming relevant again in the Panama Papers. Helga LaRouche

The FBI was completely in bed with the British. British Security Coordination, a covert operation set up by MI6 during World War II in Rockefeller Center, New York City, shown here, was the liaison between the FBI and Britain's wartime Special Operations Executive.

thought it was very significant that Jacques Attali, a prominent French economist, wrote an article this week saying, don't call them the Panama Papers, call them the London Papers. Because what this is really all about is the entire system of British offshore tax havens and Crown possessions that provide safe haven for the dark underworld of narco-terrorism, drug money laundering, and terrorism financing. If you follow the money, you can be sure that some of those threads will lead directly back to these offshore tax havens.

So as we are seeing right now, a lot of the work that has been done over years and decades by the LaRouche movement, by *Executive Intelligence Review*, by associates of Jeff Steinberg, and by Mr. LaRouche, going back to his book, *Dope, Inc.,* and also the very important film that he put out at the end of the 1990s, *Storm Over Asia,* which described exactly how these irregular warfare operations are run to destabilize countries—this work is coming together as never before. And then Mr. LaRouche's appearance on the Jack Stockwell on September 11 itself, as the attacks were occurring, that is featured in the documentary *Beyond the 28 Pages: 9/11 Ten Years Later*—the documentary from which we showed excerpts to get the statement from Mr. LaRouche earlier this evening.

If you haven't watched it, or haven't watched it lately, we would encourage you to go back and view that documentary. I think you can be ready for much, much more that will be coming from LaRouche PAC TV on this subject and its broader implications. Explore all the content that we have published on this subject in the past and share it as widely as you can with your friends and associates.

I'd like to thank Jeff Steinberg for joining us this evening. Thank you and good night.

LaRouche's 70-Year Fight Against British Terrorism

April 25—Lyndon LaRouche's fight against British-run terrorism began during his U.S. military service in India in August, 1946. He recounted it in the course of a briefing to associates on April 24, 2010.

Now, let's go back to the other part of the history, and take my particular role in this history. Well, I'm a product of World War II. I spent some time abroad during the war, in Burma, and in the post-war period, in India, for some months. My views at the time that Roosevelt died, which I had the occasion to express at the camp in Kanchrapara, which was a training depot for U.S. troops who were there—and these young fellows came up to me on the day that Roosevelt died, and said, "We want to talk to you tonight." I knew, basically, what the subject was. And when we met at dusk, off in a corner of the base, they said, "We want to know what you think is going to happen to us, now that Roosevelt is dead and Truman is President." And I said, "Well, I'm not sure, but I do know that we had a great President, under Roosevelt. And we now have a poor excuse for a President, which is Truman. And therefore, I'm afraid for us, and for our nation."

And that was sort of the beginning of my political career, because the events that I experienced later—this was at the time of Roosevelt's death—but later, coming back from northern Burma, back into Kanchrapara, and then into Calcutta, this became a bigger question. You know, I did the obvious thing that anyone would do in intelligence. (I wasn't *in* intelligence, except myself.) So, I just got into Calcutta, and went to the relevant telephone directory, and pulled up the list of all the political parties, their addresses and names, and telephone numbers, I called them up, and said I wanted—as an Ameri-

can soldier, I was interested in the future of India, and that I would like to talk to them, basically about the future India from an American standpoint.

So, I talked to all these people. They greeted me, they entertained me nicely, and I was having a grand time in Calcutta at that time, as a soldier—just the grandest time, meeting all these people, getting mixed up in all this culture and this sort of thing.

So then, the British did what the British do. There was a routine demonstration coming down the street, which was then called Dharmatala, which led to the Governor General's palace across the other side of Chowringhee. And, I met some students. There was a great trolley car station right at that intersection, they were there, and I said, "What're you up to?" And they said, "We're going on to make this demonstration at the Governor General's palace for Indian independence." I said, "Fine." And shortly after that, after they'd gone there, they were attacked by a lathi charge—you know, brass tips on a bamboo stick, which is rather nasty, because it has a whip-like effect. And they killed a few people. It had not happened recently, at that point, so obviously, this was a British provocation.

And it resulted in a large demonstration, two days later, coming down Dharmatala. Now, for the large demonstration coming down Dharmatala, which is on the other side of Chowringhee, away from the Governor's palace, the British had stationed two heavy machine guns, aimed down the street of Dharmatala. And as the crowd moved up, abreast from sidewalk to sidewalk, from building to building—massive—angry people. Hindus, Muslims, no difference. And the British opened direct fire with heavy machine

To understand the very high level of control over, and backing of, these terrorist actions (inset), we must think back to the Jacobin Terror first launched from Jeremy Bentham's London on July 14, 1789 (storming of the Bastille in Paris, above).

guns, directly into the crowd, and kept the fire going.

This resulted, two days later, in the breakout of what became the so-called "Calcutta riots." They were not riots; it was a revolution. And I was running around, calling people I knew, of these various political offices: "What's going on now? Is this going to mean a move for independence right now?"

The war was over. The Roosevelt policy was what it was, for India, even though Roosevelt was no longer there, and the intention was the development of industry. Because you had poor people, working for a few annas a day, as pay, as labor—not enough, really, to live on—working as coolies for the British Army. This kind of situation begged the creation of sovereign government, according to the Roosevelt policy. But, Truman was not Roosevelt, but quite the contrary.

And so, that was my experience. My association with these kinds of processes was defined by these events abroad, during my military service, at the end of World War II, both in Burma and India—two times in India, and once in Burma.

And I came back to the United States, and it had changed, from what I had seen when I had

lived there before, before going abroad.

January 2001 Forecast

In a Jan. 3, 2001, nationwide webcast, before George W. Bush's inauguration, LaRouche forecast a "Reichstag-fire" like terror atrocity to occur early in his term. He said:

Ashcroft was an insult to the Congress. If the Democrats in the Congress capitulate to the Ashcroft nomination, the Congress is finished.

This is pretty much like the same thing that Germany did, in February 28, 1933, when the famous *Notverordnung* (emergency decree) was established. Just remember after the Reichstag burning, the Reichstag fire, that Goering, who commanded, at that time, Prussia—he was the Minister-President of Prussia at the time—set into motion an operation. As part of this, operating under rules of Carl Schmitt, a famous pro-Nazi jurist of Germany, they passed this act called the Notverordnung, the Emergency Act, which gave the state the power, according to Schmitt's doctrine, to designate which part of his own population were enemies, and to imprison them, freely, and to eliminate them. This was the dictatorship.

Now, remember, that Hitler had come into power on January 30 of that same year—less than two months earlier. He'd come in as a minority party, which had been discredited in the previous election. He was put in by bankers, including the father of President George Bush, the former President, Prescott Bush. Prescott Bush, as agent for Harriman of New York, worked with the British banks, to put Adolf Hitler into power in January of 1933. At that time, Hitler was discredited and about to be bombed out. He was stuck into power because that was the last chance to get him in power.

Everyone said, "No, Hitler's not going to make it, because the majority of the population is against him." Then, on Feb. 28, 1933, the *Notverordnung* act was passed, on the pretext of the Reichstag's fire. And this established a dictatorship, which Germany did not get rid of until 1945.

Now, I'm not suggesting that the case of Ashcroft is comparable to the Reichstag fire. But it's a provocation, a deliberate provocation....

You don't know—We're going into a period in which either we do the kinds of things I indicated in summary to you today, or else, what you're going to have, is not a government. You're going to have something like a Nazi regime. Maybe not initially at the surface. What you're going to have is a government which cannot pass legislation, meaningful legislation. How does a government which cannot pass meaningful legislation, under conditions of crisis, govern? They govern, in every case in known history, by what's known as crisis management.

In other words, just like the Reichstag fire in Germany, How did that happen?

Well, there was a Dutchman, who was a known lunatic, and was used to set fires, as a provocateur. And he went around Germany setting fires. And one night, with no security available for the Reichstag, he went into the Reichstag building, and set the joint on fire. And Hitler came out and said, "Well, let's hope the Communists did it." And Goering moved, and the Schmitt apparatus, that is, of Carl Schmitt, the jurist. And they passed the *Notverordnung*. And on the basis of a provocation—that is, crisis management—they rammed through the *Notverordnung*, which established Hitler as dictator of Germany.

August 2001 Warning

LaRouche and his friends substantiated his warning of January. On Sept. 11, 2011, LaRouche's associates in Washington, D.C., were mass-distributing an Aug. 24 statement of his, warning of an imminent terror attack on Washington. Many of the details did not correspond to the actual Sept. 11 attacks, but the main lines were eerily precise. Its title was, "Jacobin Terror Aims at DC."

It began:

All reports from reliable sources indicate that the international terrorist movement which surfaced at Seattle, mobilized itself at Porto Alegre, Brazil, and created bloody violence at Genoa, is now taking aim at the U.S. nation's capital, Washington, D.C.....

To understand the very high level of control over and backing of these terrorist actions, even from high-level circles in governments, we must think back to the Jacobin Terror first launched from Jeremy Bentham's London on July 14, 1789. For this occasion, facing some well-documented facts from real history, in place of the usual university textbook fairy tales, will be most helpful in assisting relevant authorities to defend the security of Washington, D.C., and its environs.

After documenting the British empire's organizing of the Jacobin Terror against a threatened alliance of a republican France with the United States, the statement drew back to situate the threat of that present moment, within the world crisis.

The world is presently gripped by the biggest, most deep-going, most deadly financial and monetary crisis since Europe of the middle to late Fourteenth Century. We are in a period in which economic and related circumstances have made the idea of regular modern warfare a sick joke, in which regional and other "little wars," terrorism, political assassinations, and other forms of destabilization, are leading items on the agendas of many of the strategic planners. The financial and monetary crisis in its presently advanced stage, drives desperate political forces to the brink, desperate political forces who would rather drive civilization itself to the brink, than tolerate the changes in financial and monetary institutions which the present crisis-situation demands.

Live Interview During 9/11 Attacks

LaRouche was being interviewed live by radio host Jack Stockwell from Salt Lake City Utah, from 7:15 to 9:00 AM Mountain Time, as the 9/11 attacks unfolded.

Early in the show, Stockwell referenced the leaflet above, which LaRouche activists were distributing.

"But now, with what has just happened in New York, with this—you know, interesting enough. Just yesterday, I received—I think it was just yesterday—a bundle of leaflets from your organization in Leesburg that I regularly pass out in my office, warning of terrorist attacks in America here very shortly."

LaRouche returned to this point later, saying, "I'm not drawing any conclusions beyond what I know, because I have to be cool at this time, because I'm vindicated, in a sense. Therefore I have not got the luxury of indulging myself in any wild speculation. I have to be cool, and anything I say, I have to be right."

Lyndon H. LaRouche, Jr. (right) and Utah radio talk show host Jack Stockwell.

"The first suspicion that's going to be on this is Osama bin Laden," LaRouche said. "Is there any reason to assume this would be something other than Osama bin Laden?" Stockwell asked. "Sure," said LaRouche. "There are many. Osama bin Laden is a controlled entity. Osama bin Laden is not an independent force."

As reports came in, LaRouche and Stockwell put the picture together of the attack on the United States.

Stockwell: I want to give you a toll-free number here, where you can get some more information, relative to what we're speaking of. Ladies and gentlemen, 1-888-347-3258. 888-347-3258. Yeah, we're talking about very likely thousands of—

Witnesses are saying that they are seeing people jumping out of the World Trade Center.

LaRouche: That's a phenomenon, that is a phenomenon, that happens.

Stockwell: My God!

LaRouche: But the point is, you think about—you start with the beginning. You say, a plane comes out of Logan Airport in Boston, American Airlines. And the report, which may not be accurate, of course, is that it was hijacked after takeoff—which would make sense; I mean, that's the way something like that would tend to happen.

But there are people on that plane—you know what the size of that plane is.

Stockwell: Yes, a 767 is going to hold at least 250 people.

LaRouche: Okay, fine. So, they're going to crash into the South Tower of the World Trade Center in New York City, lower Manhattan? Already, you've got a death toll right there. A real massive one.

Now, you have the building collapse, right after the beginning of the business day, and presumably most of the employees, and a lot of other people, are going in there—you've got—you're talking about a mega-catastrophe in terms of human toll building up around this thing.

And you begin to get a pattern too. Because these things that happened, since they appear to be intentional, and the coordination suggests intention, this means it's a planned operation—it is an attack on the United States, from whom we don't know. I've got my own ideas about how this thing worked.

Document 17 and the Battle for the Truth About 9/11

by Jeffrey Steinberg

April 24—Every commissioner and key investigator into the Sept. 11, 2001 terrorist attacks on the World Trade Center and the Pentagon, in which 2,977 innocent Americans were killed, has not only demanded that President Obama declassify and publicly release the 28-page chapter from the original Joint Congressional Inquiry, providing leads on the role of the Saudi government and the Saudi Royal Family in 9/11. They have also demanded the full declassification of all of the still-classified files from the Joint Inquiry and the follow-on 9/11 Commission.

The issue is not just the 28 pages, as vital as they are. The issue is the thousands of documents that remain sealed from public view, which provide a much more in-depth picture of the magnitude of evidence against the Saudi Royals. It is the full release that is vital, and the immediate release of the 28 pages is the indispensable first step towards opening a new, top-down uninhibited probe into Saudi sponsorship of global Sunni jihad terrorism.

Such a probe will necessarily also focus on the coverup and sabotaging of the original investigations by a combination of Bush family-allied political appointees, and the larger than life role of the FBI's top management, starting with then-Director Robert Mueller, in sabotaging the probe at every turn.

This is not a matter of speculation. In July 2015, the Interagency Security Clearance Appeals Panel (ISCAP) declassified a 47-page staff working document from the 9/11 Commission, referred to as "Document 17," or "Saudi notes."

The June 6, 2003 document was written by Dana Lesemann and Michael Jacobson, two of the most important of the Federal government prosecutors and investigators assigned to the 9/11 probe. Lesemann was a Justice Department attorney and Jacobson was an FBI agent. Both were assigned to the Joint Congressional Inquiry staff and were then also hired by the 9/11 Commission to continue their earlier work. Lesemann and Jacobson conducted the investigation and contributed to the writing of the 28-page chapter of the final Joint Inquiry report. They saw their mission at the 9/11 Commission as an extension of their investigation into the Saudi role. Document 17 spelled out their ambitious plans to thoroughly probe the Saudi Royals' and Saudi government's complicity in 9/11.

FBI Coverup

Along the way, as Document 17 made clear, they ran up against serious roadblocks from the FBI, which blocked their access to key witnesses and documents, including an FBI informant in San Diego, California, code-named "Moppet," who housed two of the 9/11 hijackers and had ties to two Saudi intelligence officers who were the "handlers" of those two hijackers, Nawaf al-Hazmi and Khalid al-Mihdhar.

The 47-page June 2003 working plan made clear that the Commission and the previous Joint Inquiry had developed strong links between 21 officials of the Saudi government and the San Diego hijackers. Some of those officials were based in southern California, others were at the Saudi embassy in Washington (including a half-brother of Osama bin Laden), and others were officials of the Saudi government posted in Hamburg, Germany, where an Al-Qaeda cell was based that was intimately linked to the 9/11 team.

The tasking document also traced the southern California Saudi officials and hijackers to other cells, with key named individuals in other locations that are now known to have been central to the 9/11 attacks. These included Falls Church, Va., Paterson, N.J., Phoenix, Ariz., and Pompano Beach, Fla.

Anwar Awlaqi, a radical cleric who was subsequently killed in a President Obama-approved drone assassination attack in Yemen, was the "spiritual adviser" to the two San Diego hijackers. He moved from the San Diego mosque to a mosque in Falls Church, Va. at precisely the time that the 9/11 attackers moved to the same area in the final preparations for the attack. There are compelling reports hinting that Awlaqi himself may have had ties to the FBI while he was in the United States (Awlaqi was a natural born American citizen).

The 9/11 investigators Lesemann and Jacobson clearly came to believe that there was a systemic and top-down FBI effort to stymie the work of the Commission. A segment of Document 17, starting on page 29, details evidence of the FBI coverup and proposed remedies, including new and more intense Congressional oversight of the FBI; detailed questions and subpoenas for documents from the Bureau; and even efforts to grant Commission immunity to key witnesses who could detail the FBI duplicity. The memo makes clear that Lesemann and Jacobson saw the FBI interference as coming from the top. At one point, they candidly asked: Why did the FBI, the Justice Department, and the White House all refuse the Commission investigators access to FBI informant "Moppet," and was this indicative of a much larger FBI effort to sabotage the investigation?

Who Is the FBI Working For?

Then-FBI Director Robert Mueller had "earned his stripes" in part through his role as head of the "Get LaRouche Task Force" in the mid-1980s, which conducted the biggest political witch-hunt since the McCarthy era, targeted against the political movement led by Lyndon LaRouche. Former Attorney General of the United States Ramsey Clark called the LaRouche case the worst case of politically motivated prosecutorial abuse he had ever encountered.

Mueller's predecessor as FBI Director (Mueller took the job on Sept. 4, 2001 after serving for two months as Acting Director), Louis Freeh, subsequently became the attorney for Saudi Prince Bandar bin-Sultan, one of the highest ranking Saudi officials linked directly to the 9/11 plot. Freeh represented Bandar in matters relating to the Al-Yamamah project, which was an arms-for-oil barter deal between Britain and Saudi Arabia, negotiated by Bandar and Margaret Thatcher in 1985. The Joint Inquiry, in the 28-page chapter, linked funds from Bandar and his wife's personal account at Riggs National Bank in Washington to the two San Diego hijackers, through one of their Saudi intelligence handlers, Osama Basnan. At the time, Bandar was receiving funds from the Bank of England into his Riggs personal account, which were part of his $2 billion "commission" for his role in Al Yamamah. In his official biography, Bandar boasted that the offshore Al Yamamah funds were used for conducting covert "anti-communist" joint Anglo-Saudi intelligence operations. He openly admitted that some of those funds went to the "Afghan mujahideen." Translation: To Al Qaeda.

Document 17 makes clear that Bandar was a prime suspect in the financing of the 9/11 hijackers, and the Commission intended to probe whether Bandar and his wife, Princess Haifa, knew whether the $50-72,000 they sent to Basnan went to medical care for his wife, or for the financing of al-Hazmi and al-Mihdhar.

Document 17 was a follow-up on the solid leads and evidence that Lesemann and Jacobson included in the 28-page chapter of the original Joint Inquiry final report. It indicates the vast scope of evidence against the Saudi Royals, the in-depth infrastructure that the investigators unearthed, and the level of coverup by senior Federal officials, including the Director of the FBI himself.

Ultimately, the 9/11 Commission, like the earlier Joint Inquiry, was blocked from completing the thorough investigation the key researchers sought to pursue. At one point, staff director Philip Zelikow, who was covertly reporting the work of the Commission to then-Secretary of State Condi Rice in a scandalous conflict of interest, fired Lesemann over a conflict. That conflict began when Lesemann and Jacobson sought to obtain a copy of the 28-page chapter from the Joint Inquiry—a chapter they themselves had researched and written.

Document 17, among the 29 Commission documents declassified by ISCAP in the past 18 months, is a must-read for anyone committed to getting to the bottom of 9/11 and the coverup.

If your blood is not boiling after you read Document 17, there is something wrong with you. It offers a small window into the volumes of evidence against the Saudi Royals and the Saudi government. It should make it clear that the release of the 28 pages is an existential necessity.

The Next Phase of the Manhattan Chorus

by Diane Sare

During the Manhattan Dialogue with Lyndon La-Rouche on April 23, 2016, a military veteran from Connecticut asked the following question:

"*Good afternoon, Mr. LaRouche. It's Patrick from Greenwich, Connecticut. The 28 pages, to me, is all about the military giving their ultimate, and putting their lives on the line. This is going to be very short: Let's get the 28 pages to the public, and let's bring back our soldiers, and let's honor them. Period.*"

LaRouche: "*We need to do something a little stronger: We have to set up some kind of memorial, a living memorial for people who died in that case. That would do something. Because the United States so far has failed to do anything about that—a few handfuls of people have been concerned with that. But we have to get the humiliation expressed by the people as a whole, for their failure to defend life, human life, when that life was needed.*"

'For Us, the Living'

April 24—As Lyndon LaRouche has stressed repeatedly, after the death of the great American President Franklin Delano Roosevelt, the British empire and the Wall Street-controlled Federal Bureau of Investigation (FBI) ran a massive operation to eradicate the policies, the principles and even the memory of the Roosevelt Presidency. At the same time, they set out to destroy the principle of creativity in American politics. Americans were terrorized and told to stop thinking independently, to "go along to get along."

On September 11, 2001, with the attacks on the World Trade Center and the Pentagon, the terrorizing of the American people was taken to the most extreme level imaginable. This was a "Reichstag Fire," needed to consolidate the enslavement of the American people, and secure their passivity in the face of the looming threat of global thermonuclear war. This attack was carried out by the British empire, with the direct complic-ity of Saudi Arabia and the FBI, and the truth about those responsible has been covered up to this day.

As LaRouche stated in his remarks to the April 23 Manhattan meeting, quoted above, nothing has been done by the people of the United States to address their failure to defend those lives, or to defend the lives of countless others who have died as a result of that failure. Fifteen years after this travesty, after facing the shame of our own culpability in the current state of affairs, it is "for us, the living," as President Lincoln once said, to ensure that these people have not died in vain.

The Schiller Institute New York City Community Chorus, joined by choruses from Boston, New Jersey, and Virginia, intends to address this failure with a performance of Mozart's *Requiem* on the fifteenth anniversary of those attacks, this coming September. We will shine a beacon of truth and hope, through the genius of Mozart—to enkindle the beauty and courage which Americans today so sorely need.

Post-9/11 'Culture'

During this past week, a freight train traveled the length of Eurasia, more than 7,100 miles, from Wuhan, China to Lyon, France. It made the trip in 16 days, averaging 185 miles per hour over some of the most difficult terrain in the world. With this trip, China and her partners have opened up a vital corridor of the New Silk Road, and they have taken a step toward lifting tens of millions of people out of poverty, while simultaneously creating links of peace and economic cooperation across central Asia. Yet, almost no Americans know about this historic breakthrough.

During this same week, the rock star Prince died. Within hours every "newspaper" and media outlet in the United States was filled with front page sensational stories of his death. Twitter, Instagram, and other social media were overloaded with details, rumors, and conspiracy theories. Every American knew about this "news."

But at the same time, suicides in America are now at a thirty-year high. More and more Americans simply see no purpose in continuing, no compelling reason to continue to exist. A mistaken observer might be led to the conclusion that we are in the midst of a psychotic cultural breakdown. The truth, however, is different. What has been created since 9/11 is a Wall Street culture, erected on the shoulders of Wall Street's thievery, speculative practices, and destruction of the physical economy. It is also an FBI culture, a culture within which fear and paranoia are deliberately spread and imposed on the American People.

A Lesson from the Past

Over 600,000 Americans were killed in America's Civil War from 1861 to 1865. A significant portion of the young male population was simply wiped out, and no section of the country was left untouched by the horror. Yet, in 1867, while visiting Manhattan, the Irish-American band director, Patrick Sarsfield Gilmore, became convinced that he should organize a National Peace Jubilee as a means to unify the nation, to heal the wounds of war. The President of the United States, every Member of Congress, and all foreign dignitaries

Library of Congress/George Grantham Bain Collection

In 1867, Irish-American bank director Patrick S. Gilmore became convinced while on a trip to New York, that he should organize a National Peace Jubilee as a means to unify the nation and heal the wounds of the U.S. Civil War.

Wikipedia

A subsequent Peace Jubilee in Boston in 1872 shown here, took place after the first one, in 1869.

would be invited to attend. This should be held in a coliseum seating 50,000, in order to hold a chorus of 10,000 and an orchestra of 1,000, as well as 20,000 school children and their parents who would attend this remarkable event. Gilmore estimated that it would take about two years to prepare such a festival and, ultimately, he set June 15-17, 1869 as the date for the first National Peace Jubilee.

In March of 1869, the first circular went out by mail to choral societies and villages all over the nation soliciting their participation. It read in part, "it is desirable that where no choral societies exist, they should immediately be formed, to consist of not less than sixteen voices. As soon as such organizations are reported to us, with the number of singers upon each part, and a full list of officers, the music will be sent, bound in complete order, free of charge, and societies will be allowed to retain the same at the close of the Festival. It will be seen that in this way each society will obtain a nucleus of a library of music for choral practice without expense, and collections of choruses from the best oratorios of the great masters. In view of future similar festivals, and the improvement of the musical taste of the public generally, the awakening of a greater interest in art, and the attainment of a higher standard in sacred music, these advantages cannot be too highly estimated."

The response was overwhelming. In Boston alone, four thousand people signed up to participate in classes to learn the repertoire, and the hall for the first rehearsal was too small to hold the singers who showed up. Ultimately, over one hundred choral societies joined in the effort, *forming a chorus of 10,900 singers!* The renowned Scottish-born soprano Euphrosyne Parepa-Rosa led the training of the choruses, and sang as the

Wikipedia

Euphrosyne Parepa-Rosa

View of the great coliseum for the World's Peace Jubilee and International Musical Festival, 1872.

leading soloist at the event. She had an extraordinary range, and such placement that her voice carried effortlessly to every corner of the vast coliseum. The choral repertoire included several choruses each from Haydn's *Creation,* Handel's *Messiah,* and Mendelssohn's *Elijah,* as well as Rossini's *Stabat Mater.*

Needles to say, the Jubilee was a rousing and inspiring success in every intended way. President Ulysses S. Grant addressed the gathering on the second day and was greeted with overflowing enthusiasm. A verse was added to the national anthem, appropriate to the occasion and its intent: the unity of the United States of America:

> *Not as North, nor as South, in the future*
> *she'll stand, But as brothers united throughout*
> *this broad land. And the Star Spangled Banner*
> *forever shall wave O'er the land of the free*
> *and the home of the brave.*

Seven years later, at the 1876 Centennial Exposition held in Philadelphia, a chorus of 1,000 voices performed George Frideric Handel's "Hallelujah Chorus" from the *Messiah.* Where did this chorus come from? Was this music just an ornament on a display of industrial and scientific prowess from a young republic? Immediately following this performance of the "Hallelujah Chorus," President Ulysses Grant and Dom Pedro, the Emperor of Brazil (the first foreign head of state to visit the United States) walked over to start the giant Corliss Engine, which was the power generator for the entire exposition.

The Centennial Exposition of 1876 grew directly out of the impact of the earlier Jubilee, but the origins of both go back even earlier. Aided by the influx of continental European and Irish immigrants, choral music, with a special emphasis on Italian bel canto placement, had come to dominate American culture by the Nineteenth Century. The largest and best known of these choral groups was the Handel and Haydn Society, which had been founded in 1815 and received a great boost in the 1850s when Germania, an orchestra of German immigrants, joined with them, dramatically raising the level of what they could accomplish. The Handel and Haydn Society chorus grew to 500 singers, and members of the Germania group became some of their finest directors.

Returning to our Mission

Today, Lyndon LaRouche has singled out Manhattan, the city of Alexander Hamilton, as the point of origin for a new American Renaissance, a renaissance which will pull our presently impoverished and stupefied population out of the legendary "Slough of Despond," into the potentials of a Science Century, as we collaborate with China and Russia in transforming the world for the benefit of all mankind.

The planned performance of Mozart's *Requiem* on and around September 11, 2016, the fifteenth anniversary of the murderous attack on our Republic, is designed to do the same. The process of building the chorus as we approach that date is at least as important as the performance itself. It is clear that if we can succeed in creating the 1,500 person chorus that Mr. LaRouche called for about a year ago, we will create the conditions in which a great evil, namely the events of September 11, 2001, can be looked back upon as the moment that we changed our ways, and decided to *return to the true mission of our Republic*—to uphold the dignity and sanctity of human life, as above and apart from mere beasts. It is this quality of immortality that a dying Mozart captured in the sublime power of his *Requiem,* and in this way, those people who gave the "ultimate" will have been able to also contribute an enduring good for the future of this nation and all mankind.

The Leibnizian Roots of Eurasian Integration

by Jason Ross[1]

Since 1996, the LaRouche movement has been organizing for the realization of continental development of Eurasia and beyond, under the programs of, first, the Eurasian Land-Bridge, and now the New Silk Road and World Land-Bridge.[2] This economic approach was championed three centuries earlier by the prolific polymath and economist, Gottfried Wilhelm Leibniz (1646-1716), who worked to open up the potential for exchange of goods and ideas with China, and to modernize Russia, economically and scientifically. Leibniz encapsulated his outlook in the preface to his *News from China*:

> I consider it a singular plan of the fates that human cultivation and refinement should today be concentrated, as it were, in the two extremes of our continent, in Europe and in China, which adorns the Orient as Europe does the opposite edge of the Earth. Perhaps Supreme Providence has ordained such an arrangement, so that as the most cultivated and distant peoples stretch out their arms to each other, those in between may gradually be brought to a better way of life. I do not think it an accident that the Russians, whose vast realm connects Europe with China and who hold sway over the deep barbarian lands of the North by the shore of the frozen ocean, should be led to the emulation of our ways through the strenuous efforts of their present ruler [Peter I].[3]

Gottfried Wilhelm Leibniz (1646-1716), the beautifully optimistic polymath who, three hundred years ago, set the conceptual groundwork for the programs of international cooperation and development being realized today, thanks to the efforts of the LaRouche movement.

Leibniz saw the goal of society as advancing the knowledge of the world to contribute to the public good, and to glorify God by better understanding His wisdom in His having acted as He has:

> To contribute to the public good and to the glory of God is the same thing. It seems that the aim of all humankind should chiefly be nothing other

---

1. The author is presenting a series of video discussions on the life and work of Gottfried Leibniz, available at: http://lpac.co/leibniz-2016

2. See *EIR*'s 2014 special report, *The New Silk Road Becomes the World Land-Bridge*, at worldlandbridge.com

3. G.W. Leibniz, Preface to the *Novissima Sinica* (*News from China*), translated by Daniel J. Cook and Henry Rosemont, Jr., in *Gottfried Wilhelm Leibniz: Writings on China*, Open Court, 1998, pp. 45–46.

than the knowledge and development of the wonders of God and that it is for this reason that God has given to humankind dominion over this globe.[4]

China: the Work of the Missionaries

What were the relations of Europe with China in Leibniz's time? From Roman times, nearly a millennium passed without significant direct contact between Europe and China, until the trip of Marco Polo, preceded by his father and uncle. His *Travels of Marco Polo*, circa 1300, was the first major European chronicle of the East. In the 1510s, Europeans made their first sea voyages to China.

In 1549, Francis Xavier, who was one of the founders of the Society of Jesus—the Jesuit order—arrived in Asia to begin a *commerce of light*, as Leibniz called it, with the cultures there, where he planned to evangelize, and also to learn from the Chinese and others. As the missions worked to develop an understanding of Chinese language and culture, Father Matteo Ricci (1552-1610) arrived in 1582. Before departing on his voyage, Ricci had worked on science, language, geometry, astronomy, and music, being instructed by the famous mathematician and astronomer Christopher Clavius. Ricci came to China prepared to really offer something to the Chinese.

Clearly, as a Jesuit, his primary focus was to evangelize, and teach Christianity, but that was not his sole mission. The situation in China was nothing like the kind of work that missionaries had been involved in, in other parts of the world, such as parts of Africa, or in the New World. The Chinese culture had a conscious knowledge of its own history that dated back to before the Biblical Flood, without any record of it.[5] This was an *old* culture.

In his studies, Ricci found that some of the ideas about how China worked that were considered common knowledge in Europe, were actually incorrect. One of them was the idea of the "three religions": that Buddhism, Daoism, and Confucianism had merged into one outlook, or that the three, considered as a hodgepodge combination, together constituted Chinese thought. By actually studying those belief systems, Ricci found that

Matteo Ricci (1552-1610), the Jesuit missionary and scientist whose approach to the Chinese—one of accommodation and mutual learning—was referred back to by both Leibniz and the Kangxi Emperor as a model for cultural exchange.

this was not true, that these were different systems of thought.

There wasn't simply an "Eastern," or a "Chinese" philosophy, just as there is no single "Western" philosophy. It is not only in the West that there are thinkers with different viewpoints. Although Plato and Aristotle might be near each other in the bookstore, that doesn't mean that their thoughts are aligned; they are not! The same thing is true in China; there is a long history of different outlooks, of different types of thought.

So Ricci's view was to bring science, and the fruits of science, to China, both for evangelization purposes, and because this is simply something that all people should know. All peoples should be able to benefit from the breakthroughs of the Renaissance, whose science should be brought out to the world. Such was Ricci's outlook. Ricci taught geometry. He translated what he

---

4. Maria Rosa Antognazza, *Leibniz: An Intellectual Biography*, Cambridge University Press, 2009, p. 233.

5. This was a bit of a mystery to the missionaries.

considered to be great works into Chinese. He taught music. He presented the court of the emperor with a harpsichord. He wrote music for the Chinese court, including songs for multiple voices. For Ricci, as for Leibniz, science and religion did not in any way stand counterposed to each other.

As an example of this unified approach of religion and science, consider Leibniz's discussion, in his *Discourse on Metaphysics,* on the reason for God's actions being praiseworthy.[6] Were these actions good by virtue of God having done them (an expression only of God's power), or did he act as he did *because doing so was good* (an expression of God's wisdom and goodness).[7] Leibniz knew that the latter was true. While some philosophers saw the supposed limitation on His power as contradicting His omnipotence, Leibniz considered the basis of leadership of a great prince to be similar: One justifies one's rule by doing good. There is no contradiction between reason (as in science) and religion, in his view.

Regarding a potential stumbling block, Ricci wrote that Confucianism wasn't a religion. It was an ethical system, based on the existence of natural law. He wrote that Confucius was not worshipped as a god, but was praised "for the good teachings that he left in his books … without, however, reciting any prayers nor asking for any favor."[8] People did not pray to Confucius to intercede in worldly affairs. This is respect for an honored thinker. Ricci found that this also applied to the honoring of ancestors, or the great thinkers of the past—the ancient masters.

Ricci wrote that, as for the veneration of ancient masters and one's ancestors, these rites were to "display the gratitude of the living as they cherish the rewards of Heaven, and to excite men to perform actions which render them worthy of the recognition of posterity."[9]

This is a beautiful description of an efficient sense of immortality: By recognizing—venerating—the good deeds of the past, one demonstrates that posterity's *future judgment* is something that exists efficiently *in the present.* Culturally, there is a profound value in this outlook, which could be strengthened by rites and social practices that reinforce the concept.

Ricci differentiated Confucianism from Buddhism and Daoism, which he did see as religions. If Chinese were not Buddhists or Daoists, he said, then they "could certainly become Christians, since the essence of their doctrine contains nothing contrary to the essence of the Catholic faith, nor would the Catholic faith hinder them in any way, but would indeed aid in that attainment of the quiet and peace of the republic which their books claim as their goal."[10]

The work of Ricci and his allies met with great success. His differentiation among the different currents of religious and philosophical thought in China allowed him to understand the culture, and to intervene in it—to bring new thoughts to it—in a refined and specific way. In 1644, the Qing dynasty came to power, replacing the Ming dynasty. Throughout the changes, the missionaries stayed and continued their work. The first of the new Qing emperors made the Jesuits his son's tutors. And that son became the Kangxi Emperor, a remarkable ruler. He was the first to compile the characters of the Chinese language, in the Kangxi dictionary. He promoted science and upgraded the Beijing Observatory with the assistance of the Jesuit scientist Ferdinand Verbiest. His interest in music led him to learn to play the keyboard. An advocate of learning, he maintained the meritocratic examination system even during difficult times, and issued an edict requiring, in every town, the posting and reading of a set of Confucian maxims that he wrote.

The success of the missionaries was manifest in a decision by the emperor in 1692, the Edict of Toleration, granting Christians the right to go throughout the Chinese Empire to teach, preach, and visit, and to have their churches protected, as long as they did not undermine Confucian principles and the ceremonies and rites that were required of civil servants. The Kangxi Emperor saw no contradiction between Christianity and the Confucian principles that were the foundation of Chinese society.

Opposition to the 'Commerce of Light'

In Europe, the progress in cultural and economic exchange with China was not entirely met with approval. The oligarchical outlook in Europe opposed this exchange for two reasons. First, the spreading of science and economic progress is generally opposed by an oli-

---

6. Leibniz, *Discourse on Metaphysics,* various translations, Articles 2-3.
7. See also Leibniz's arguments in the *Leibniz-Clarke Correspondence.*
8. As quoted in Michael Billington, "Christians Must Know what Confucius Said," *EIR,* Volume 18 Number 19, May 17, 1991, p. 50.
9. Ibid.

---

10. As quoted in Michael Billington, "Matteo Ricci, the Grand Design, and the Disaster of the 'Rites Controversy,'" *EIR,* Volume 28 Number 43, Nov. 9, 2001, p. 41.

The Kangxi Emperor (1654-1722), during whose reign Leibniz intervened into relations between Europe and China. The Emperor was a great supporter of learning, and welcomed the participation of missionaries in China with the 1692 Edict of Toleration.

arrive at truth through reason, undermines the notion of authority as the arbiter of what is right and wrong.

For these two reasons (among others), there was an attempt—unfortunately one that would prove to be ultimately successful—to end this *commerce of light*, this exchange between Europe and China.

Enter Leibniz

It was in this setting that Leibniz's involvement began. Let's start with Leibniz's view of the ruler of China at the time, the Kangxi Emperor. Leibniz wrote of him that he is a monarch "who almost exceeds human heights of greatness, being a god-like mortal, ruling by a nod of his head, who, however, is educated to virtue and wisdom ... thereby earning the right to rule."[11] In writing of his having "earned the right to rule," Leibniz expresses his view of real leadership, based not (solely) on power, but on goodness and wisdom, reflecting his view of God and the universe.

Despite the congruent conceptions of natural law in China and Europe, a controversy around the Confucian rites was used to kill off the cultural exchange with China. Some missionaries and factions in the Catholic Church said that it was not possible to be both Confucian and Christian, and each individual would have to decide one way or the other. The attitude was that those venerating their ancestors or Confucius were engaging in heathen, inherently un-Christian behavior. One of these missionaries, Antonio de St. Marie, said, "We have come here to announce the Holy Gospel, and not to be apostles of Confucius."[12] That's the heavy-handed approach that they had.

And again, they could ask of themselves, how could it be that in China, "an empire so vast, so enlightened, established so solidly, and so flourishing ... in number of inhabitants and in invention of almost all the arts, the Divinity has never been acknowledged?"[13] What does it mean, that a society can flourish in that way, on a set of principles other than those that these missionaries had come to expect from their history in Europe? Leibniz says that this shows that there is a sense of reason that is impressed in all people of the world, that can lead them to the right kinds of conclusions—that there is a universality in humanity.

So, what did Leibniz do? He wrote a series of papers

garchical leadership, hoping to keep people in a general state of ignorance and poverty. Secondly, the natural theology of the Chinese—whereby, without divine revelation, human beings are able to come to meaningful conclusions about immortality and the nature of the universe—threatens the status of authority in matters of thought.

Consider the prototypical oligarch, the Zeus of the Promethean tale, who forbade the use of fire by human beings, reserving such knowledge and power to himself. For a ruler of Zeusian outlook, the promotion of science in China is a very bad idea, as its economic effects would also serve to make it more difficult to maintain control over society. Similarly, the idea that individuals can

11. Billington, Ibid., p. 39.

12. Ibid., p. 40.

13. Ibid.

and reports in which he weighs in on these matters. They are available in English translation.[14] In his Preface to his *News from China*, Leibniz writes:[15]

But if this process [this exchange of thought] should be continued I fear that we may soon become inferior to the Chinese in all branches of knowledge. I do not say this because I grudge them new light; rather I rejoice. But it is desirable that they in turn teach us those things which are especially in our interest: the greatest use of practical philosophy and a more perfect manner of living, to say nothing now of their other arts. Certainly the condition of our affairs [in Europe], slipping as we are into ever greater corruption, seems to be such that we need missionaries from the Chinese who might teach us the use and practice of natural religion, just as we have sent them teachers of revealed theology. And so I believe that if someone expert, not in the beauty of goddesses, but in the excellence of peoples, were selected as judge, the golden apple would be awarded to the Chinese unless we should win by virtue of one great but superhuman thing, namely, the divine gift of the Christian religion.[16]

Leibniz believes that in terms of *natural* theology, of thoughts that did not derive from the revealed theology of Christianity, the Chinese are ahead.

Consider what he writes here about the emperor, and the concept of what it means to be the ruler. Contrast Leibniz's outlook with that of Thomas Hobbes, or the Thrasymachus of Plato's *Republic*. Leibniz writes:

Nor is it easy to find anything worthier of note than the fact that this greatest of kings, who possesses such complete authority in his own day, anxiously fears posterity and is in greater dread of the judgment of history, than other kings are of representatives of estates and parliaments. Therefore he carefully seeks to avoid actions which might cast a reflection upon his reputation

when recorded by the chroniclers of his reign and placed in files and secret archives.[17]

This is the value of respecting the past, as a way of thinking of one's own life, as the future's past. The emperor, although temporally (and temporarily) powerful, fears the judgment of posterity, more than a European king might fear the power of the Parliament. In Leibniz's view, this shows the value of natural law in Chinese culture.

Leibniz weighs in on what he called "The Civil Cult of Confucius," discussing the rites used to revere Confucius's life:

When I wrote the Preface to my *News from China*, I was inclined to believe that when the Chinese literati render honors to Confucius, they consider it a civil ceremony rather than a religious cult. Since then, an opposing statement has come into my hands, published by people, who though deemed well-intentioned, have not at all persuaded me [of their view].[18]

The "opposing statement" Leibniz refers to is the growing anti-Chinese faction in the church. Leibniz continues:

A religious cult, is one where we attribute to he whom we honor, a superhuman power, capable of granting us rewards or inflicting punishments on us.[19]

This is clearly not something that people think about Confucius! Leibniz goes on:

For example, when they call the place where the image of the deceased is displayed and to whom gifts are offered a "throne" or a "seat" of the soul or spirit, this can be easily understood in an anthropomorphic or poetic fashion, as describing the glory attributed to immortality, and not as if they think the soul actually returns to this place and rejoices in the offerings.[20]

14. G.W. Leibniz, *Gottfried Wilhelm Leibniz: Writings on China*, translated by Daniel J. Cook and Henry Rosemont, Jr., Open Court, 1998.
15. The *Novissima Sinica* (*News from China*) was a collection of letters and reports from Leibniz's correspondents, with a Preface written by Leibniz himself, published in 1697 and 1699.
16. *Writings on China*, pp. 50-51.
17. Ibid., p. 48.
18. Leibniz, "On the Civil Cult of Confucius," 1700/1701, *Writings on China*, p. 61.
19. Ibid.
20. Ibid., p. 62.

The value of these ceremonies lies in inculcating a sense of the present as what will be the future's past, not in the benefits to departed souls being worshipped in that way.

In fact, Leibniz points out something very similar in the Bible. He remarks that honoring ancestors is hardly unique to China, and he cites the Fifth Commandment: "Honor your father and your mother, that your days may be long upon the land, which the Lord your God has given you." Leibniz says that it is not directly by honoring one's parents that one lives longer, but that the kind of thought that goes along with it, is something that God rewards for other reasons.

In describing the Confucian view of one of the words you might say is "heaven," Leibniz writes, in a powerful statement on the value of the natural theology of the Chinese:

> They sacrifice to this visible Heaven (or rather to its King) and revere in profound silence that *Li*[21] which they do not name, because of the ignorance, or the vulgarity of the people, who would not understand the nature of the *Li*. What we call the light of reason in man, they call commandment and law of heaven. What we call the inner satisfaction of obeying justice and our fear of acting contrary to it, all this is called by the Chinese (and by us as well) inspirations sent by the *Xangti*[22] (that is, by the true God). To offend heaven is to act against reason, to ask pardon of heaven is to reform oneself and to make a sincere return in word and deed in submission one owes to this very law of reason. For me I find all this quite excellent, and quite in accord with *natural theology*. Far from finding any distorted understanding here, I believe that it is only by strained interpretations and by interpolations that one could find anything to criticize on this point. It is pure Christianity, insofar as it renews the natural law inscribed in our hearts—except for what revelation and grace add to it to improve our nature.[23]

---

21. The *Li* Leibniz is referring to is likely 理, meaning "reason," "order," or "principle."
22. Leibniz's spelling of Shàngdì (上帝).
23. Leibniz, "Discourse on the Natural Philosophy of the Chinese," 1716, *Writings on China*, p. 105. Leibniz's emphasis.

The Kangxi Emperor updated the Beijing Observatory with the help of such missionary scientists as Father Ferdinand Verbiest.

Leibniz takes the time to go through these issues in detail, because it was essential to defuse the attempt to prevent the relationship with China from developing and continuing.

A Reversal

Regrettably, Leibniz's work did not succeed, at least not in his time.

In 1704, Pope Clement XI issued a decree, and then a papal bull in 1715, saying that anyone who wanted to be considered a Christian would have to renounce the Chinese rites: no ceremonies for Confucius, no reverence of ancestors. The Kangxi Emperor, who had been taught in his youth by Jesuits, and had in 1692 given the Christian missionaries free rein throughout the kingdom, could not abandon these Confucian rites, and could not accept the papal bull, without overturning the

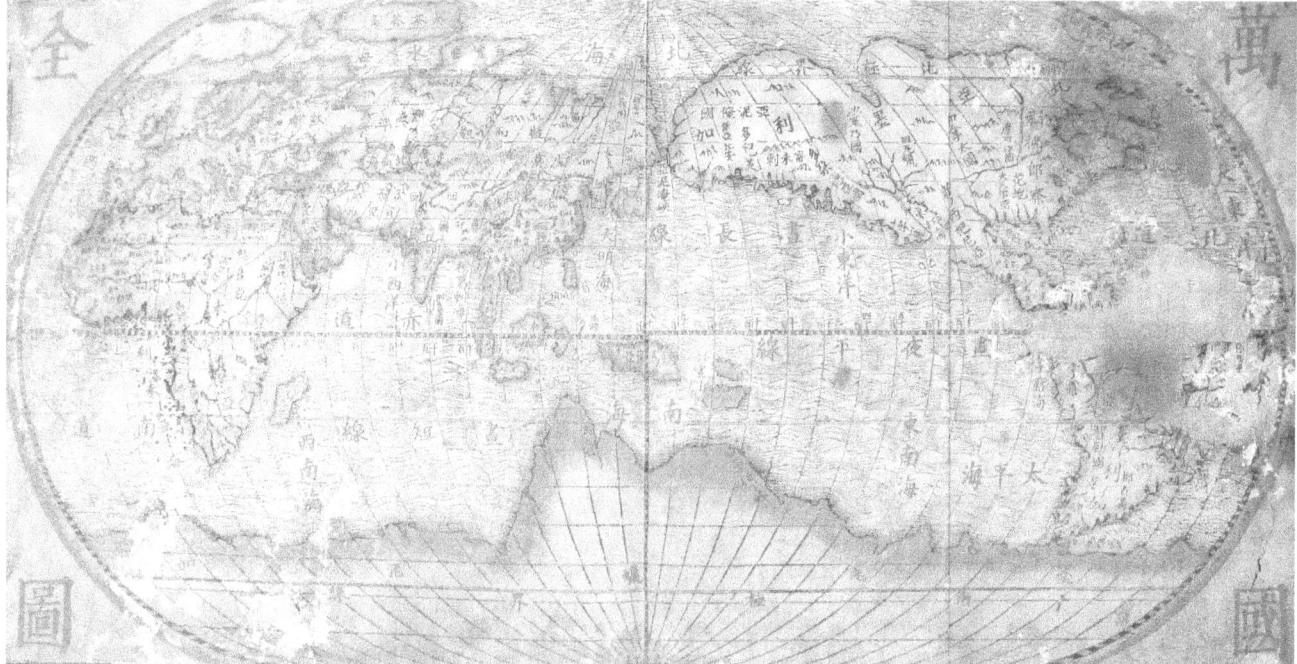

This world map, dating from the early 1600s and labelled in Chinese, was prepared by the Jesuit missionary and scholar Giulio Alenio. The "commerce of light," as Leibniz called the exchange with China, had the potential to expand the knowledge both of the Chinese and Europeans.

basis of Chinese society. Under the Chinese meritocratic system, civil servants were all required to take examinations, a significant aspect of which included a grounding in the ancient philosophy of Confucius and others. To abandon this would be to overthrow the Chinese Constitution, not in a paper or written sense, but in the intellectual sense of overthrowing the principles on which the nation operated.

The Kangxi Emperor explained this to the representatives from the Vatican who came to speak to him. He clarified that his philosophy agreed with the existence of one omnipotent deity who created and who rules the world, and that the rites regarding ancestors and Confucius were signs of veneration, but were not religious. He was clear that the Chinese were not asking for their ancestors or Confucius to intercede into the world.

The emperor's explanations were unsuccessful. When the papal representatives returned to him with the announcement that the Vatican was taking a position that would have the effect of ending the cultural exchange, the emperor responded:

You have corrupted your teachings, and you have disrupted the efforts of the former Westerners. This is definitely not the will of your God, for He leads men to good deeds. I have often heard from you Westerners that the devil leads men astray—this must be it.[24]

The emperor further remarked that most of the missionaries who came and made judgments about China's theology, had never even learned Chinese, in contrast to Matteo Ricci, who had translated Chinese works. Leibniz himself strongly promoted a large-scale translation project, to really understand the different philosophies in China, as a real exchange, writing: "I only wish that we had more complete accounts and greater quantity of extracts of the Chinese classics accurately translated which talk about first principles. Indeed, it would even be desirable that all the classics be translated together."[25]

Leibniz tried to intervene through the end of his life. When he passed away in 1716, he was still working on his "Discourse on the Natural Theology of the Chinese," unable to finish it as he labored away on the history of the Guelf family for King George. After Leib-

24. Billington, "Matteo Ricci, the Grand Design, and the Disaster of the 'Rites Controversy,'" p. 41.
25. "Discourse on the Natural Philosophy of the Chinese," in *Writings on China*, p. 78.

niz's death, another papal bull issued by Pope Benedict XIV in 1742 reaffirmed the earlier bull and forbade any discussion of the policy. Missionaries would have to swear an oath that they would not even discuss the justification of the church's position. If they wanted to go to China, they were not allowed to even discuss the idea that Confucianism was coherent with Christianity.

The exchange was effectively ended. The toleration of the practice of Christianity and of missionary work, allowed under the emperor's 1692 edict, was ended. Most Westerners left, losing the opportunity to benefit from China's history and culture, and China was cut off from the science, technology, and culture that the exchange could have brought, something that was certainly in Britain's favor later in the opium wars of the 19th Century.

This outcome did not result from religious zealotry or firmly sticking to theological principles on the part of some missionaries. The theological debate was used to prevent the political and economic results that would arise from a closer cooperation with China, and through an exchange of thought—in economic science and other fields. The papal bulls were only overturned in 1939, when Pope Pius XII finally acknowledged that it was possible to be both a Confucian, including observing rites of respect, and a Christian, as was, for example, Sun Yat-sen.

Consider again Leibniz's view of the great potential of exchange with China, and compare it with the small-mindedness of those who got pulled into the religious debate, and the evil intent of those who promoted it from the top:

> I judge that this mission is the greatest affair of our time, as much for the glory of God and the propagation of the Christian religion as for the general good of men and the growth of the arts and sciences, among us as well as among the Chinese. For this is a commerce of light, which could give to us at once their work of thousands of years and render ours to them, and double, so to speak, our true wealth for one and the other. This is something greater than one imagines.[26]

This is indeed greater than one could imagine. What might the world be like today, had that exchange continued, had those attempts to prevent the exchange with China not succeeded?

Russia

Recall Leibniz's thought that it almost seemed to be God's intention to have Europe and China on opposite ends of the Continent, each to reach towards the other with its own outlook, science, and civilization. Now, consider what he saw as Russia's role:

> I do not think it an accident that the Russians, whose vast realm connects Europe with China and who hold sway over the deep barbarian lands of the North by the shore of the frozen ocean, should be led to the emulation of our ways through the strenuous efforts of their present ruler [Peter I].

That "present ruler" of Russia, Tsar Peter I (Peter the Great), was someone with whom Leibniz met personally on more than one occasion. Beyond the desire to reach China by land, rather than by sea, Leibniz saw a great deal of promise for Russia itself. Peter the Great wanted to develop his nation, to move it forward economically and culturally. He wanted to bring in science. He wanted to modernize.

He was also personally very excited about getting a hands-on sense of industries and the technical arts. In 1697 he came to Europe in a personal rather than official capacity[27] to study shipbuilding and other sorts of industry, with a particular goal of touring the shipyards of Holland. He was assisted in setting up this trip by the daughter of the previous Duke of Hanover, Sophie Charlotte, who was a student of Leibniz, and who had married the Elector of Brandenburg. Sophie Charlotte helped bring Peter the Great into Europe. And on his way to Holland, Peter the Great stopped in Hanover, where he was hosted by Sophie Charlotte's mother, the Electress Sophie, another supporter of Leibniz, and who was to become next in line to inherit the throne of England, thanks in part to Leibniz's work on the 1701 Act of Settlement.

For his industrial tour of Europe in 1697, Peter the Great was thus brought in by an ally of Leibniz, and hosted at the home of another ally of Leibniz. During

---

26. Letter to the Jesuit missionary Antoine Verjus, Dec. 2, 1697, as quoted by Maria Rosa Antognazza in her *Leibniz: An Intellectual Biography*, p. 359, from the translation by Franklin Perkins in "Leibniz's Exchange with the Jesuits in China," in Paul Lodge (ed.), *Leibniz and his Correspondents*, Cambridge University Press, 2004.

---

27. To avoid publicity, he travelled under an assumed name.

this trip, Leibniz attempted to meet with the Tsar, which he was unable to do, having to content himself with meeting members of his court. One of their topics of discussion was the history of the Russian language, about which Leibniz had some insights.

The big break really came in the 1710s. Another one of Leibniz's employer-patrons, Duke Anton Ulrich, a relative of the Hanoverians who were Leibniz's main employers, was to celebrate the marriage of one of his granddaughters to the Tsar's oldest son.[28] When the Tsar came to Germany for the wedding, the Duke asked Leibniz if he would like to come to the wedding, which, naturally, Leibniz was very happy to do.

And so in October 1711, Leibniz was able to personally meet with the Tsar. To this meeting he brought reports on mapping Russia, on studying its mineral resources, on its linguistic history, on how to approach a study of its history, and proposals for setting up societies for the advancement of science and technology and modernizing the economy. Leibniz came prepared! In a follow-up letter after their meeting, Leibniz wrote to the Tsar in 1712:

> Although I have very frequently been employed in public affairs and also in the judiciary system and am consulted on such matters by great princes on an ongoing basis, I nevertheless regard the arts and the sciences as a higher calling, since through them the glory of God and the best interests of the whole human race are continuously promoted. For in the sciences and the knowledge of nature and art, the wonders of God, his power, wisdom, and goodness are especially manifest; and the arts and sciences are also the true treasury of the human race, through which art masters nature and civilized peoples are distinguished from barbarian ones. For these reasons I have loved and pursued science since my youth.... The one thing I have been lacking is a leading prince who adequately embraced this cause.... I am not a man devoted solely to his native country, or to one particular nation: On the contrary, I pursue the interests of the whole human race because I regard heaven as my fatherland and all well-meaning

Tsar Peter the Great (1672-1725) developed Russia economically, scientifically, and culturally. His meetings with Leibniz in the 1710s bore fruit in such institutions as the St. Petersburg Academy of Sciences.

> people as its fellow citizens.... To this aim, for a long time I have been conducting a voluminous correspondence in Europe, and even as far as China; and for many years I have not only been a fellow of the French and English Royal Societies but also direct, as president, the Royal Prussian Society of Sciences.[29]

Leibniz was making himself available as an adviser to the Tsar, and made the point that the pursuit and promotion of science and technology, to understand the wonders of nature and to better the life of human beings, requires government support. Leibniz is asking whether the Tsar will step up and provide that kind of support.

In 1712, Leibniz had a series of follow-up meetings with the Tsar, during the Tsar's visit to Germany. Leib-

_____

28. The granddaughter, Charlotte Christine, had an elder sister, Elizabeth Christine, who had married Charles VI, the Holy Roman Emperor, providing another connection between Leibniz and the imperial court of Vienna.

_____

29. As quoted in Antognazza, *Leibniz: An Intellectual Biography*, pp. 470-471.

niz traveled with him to several cities as part of his entourage, allowing them to continue their discussions.

As a result of his meetings, Leibniz was appointed a member of the Russian government, becoming a Russian privy councilor of justice. He became the adviser to the Tsar on mathematics and science, and was given the task of reforming the judicial system of Russia, which Leibniz said made him feel like Solon of Athens. Although Leibniz was to pass away only a few years later, without the opportunity to fully realize his plans during this lifetime, his influence was significant. Consider some of the achievements:

In 1725, the Academy of Sciences of St. Petersburg was set up in that new city named after Tsar Peter I. A new advisory body, a Senate, was set up for the government. Leibniz's proposals to reorganize the government resulted in the consolidation of the then 35 government departments into nine.[30] The number of iron foundries during the reign of Peter quadrupled. By 1725, a dozen years after Leibniz's meetings with the Tsar, Russia had matched England's iron output. By 1785, Russia was producing more iron than all the rest of Europe combined. This was a very successful and quite rapid industrialization. Before Peter's reforms, Russia had been relatively backward in comparison with the cultural centers of Europe.

During the American War of Independence, it was a member of that Leibniz-created Academy of Sciences who drafted the agreement of the League of Armed Neutrality, the anti-British agreement to prevent interference with international trade, prominently including trade with America during the war.

Conclusion

Leibniz's universal outlook led him to extend his interests and influence around the world. He sought to develop ties to China—for extending trade, skills, and knowledge—believing that Europe could learn from Chinese philosophy. He wanted to extend the fruits of what had been learned in Europe to other cultures, so those discoveries could be implemented to improve people's lives, and be developed further by thinkers in other parts of the world. He saw Russia both as a link with China and as an important developing and potentially very powerful nation. He thought it could actually be a benefit that Russia was entering the world of modern science as late as it was, since many bad ideas could perhaps be avoided entirely in Russia, where new scientific academies could be set up, unburdened by unfruitful outlooks.

His relationships with these two countries represented Leibniz's optimistic drive to improve the world, based on what is universal to all nations. Again, Leibniz:

> I judge that this mission is the greatest affair of our time, as much for the glory of God and the propagation of the Christian religion as for the general good of men and the growth of the arts and sciences, among us as well as among the Chinese. For this is a commerce of light, which could give to us at once their work of thousands of years and render ours to them, and double, so to speak, our true wealth for one and the other. This is something greater than one imagines.[31]

Considering the potential today, with the New Silk Road proposals—the Chinese One Belt One Road program, the World Land-Bridge developed by Lyndon and Helga LaRouche and their collaborators, the Asian Infrastructure Investment Bank, the BRICS process, and the Chinese space program—it is undeniable that there is a great potential, a commerce of light that the entire world must be allowed to join. This requires eliminating the power of that greatest of impediments standing in the way: the trans-Atlantic financial outlook that stands opposed to such development—that Wall Street, London, banking, oligarchical, anti-development, anti-technology, anti-cooperation outlook.

The people of the United States stand in a position of great responsibility, to ensure that our nation, through its actions under its current President—who must be removed—does not prevent this kind of development from occurring; indeed, we should be participating in today's "commerce of light." As a nation, the United States can do much to advance these kinds of proposals in the context of a national mission for development. We have a great deal of work to do.

Leibniz's approach to the relations among nations, the purpose of an individual nation, and the purpose of relations between them, between different cultures, provides a very valuable framework, a historical anchor point for how to relate to each other today. Leibniz made progress, but it is up to us today to realize his program for continental development and collaboration.

---

30. Apparently, Russian bureaucracy is nothing new.

31. Antognazza, p. 359.

The Importance of Riemann Today

by Bruce Director

April 23—Bernhard Riemann's habilitation dissertation—see *The Importance of Bernhard Riemann by Bruce Director, EIR March 25, 2016*—is the most famous expression, and most accessible to the non-scientist, of Riemann's revolutionary discoveries. But citizens wishing to understand and act on the crucial matters of politics, economics, and science that will determine whether Mankind survives the current crisis, would be well advised to acquaint themselves with the broader scope of Riemann's work.

In doing so, you will find many wonderful results that have laid the foundation for virtually every important development in science for the last century and a half, but even more important, an insight into a creative thinker who recognized, in his own creativity itself, the principles on which the organization of the universe is based. It is that quality of thinking that the world is in such need today.

I will give several examples to illustrate the point just made, beginning with Riemann's earliest published work.

By the time Riemann came to Göttingen to study with Gauss in 1846, he had already concluded that any new discovery in science must come from rooting out the stultifying method of thinking that had become dominant in Germany since the rise of Immanuel Kant. Gauss had already recognized this and in his early years took it on quite aggressively, but after the rise of Napoleon and the subsequent reaction, he had kept much of his thinking under wraps.

Kant had reintroduced Aristotle's separation of mind from the universe as a reaction against the great achievements of Gottfried Leibniz, in an attempt to seal off science from creative thinking. According to Kant's dictum, pure thinking could only proceed by a set of rules abstracted from all reality outside the mind. Hence, protected from the unruly world of material things and the unreliable world of sense perception, a system of pure reason could be constructed that was reliable.

The problem was that such a system was as impotent as it was useless. This didn't bother Kant, who developed a system of practical reason and other compromises to deal with the real world, as long as the world was made orderly by a controlling oligarchy (either human or deified). It nevertheless served to put a constraint on creative thinking in science, art and politics, which, fortunately, was disrupted by Six Prometheans such as Wolfgang Amadeus Mozart, Ludwig van Beethoven, Friedrich Schiller, Franz Schubert, Abraham Gotthelf Kästner, and Karl Friedrich Gauss.

From Leibniz to Riemann

The seemingly most secure refuge for Kantianism was pure mathematics, and within that domain, algebra and number theory,— as these, Kant insisted, were creations of pure reason, and could not be polluted by the unmanageable world of matter and mind. But lurking in this world of pure logic was an unwelcome spirit, the square root of -1, that had so bedeviled the inner sanctum of pure reason that it had earned for itself the appellation, *impossible* or *imaginary*.[1]

The reality was that the square root of -1 isn't impossible. It shows up repeatedly in the system of algebra or number.[2] It was only "impossible" because its meaning was in the real world, not the abstract world of pure reason. Gauss insisted that like negative numbers, the concept of "imaginary" numbers was not derived by

---

1. Denoted by the letter i.
2. For example, the abstract algebraic expression x^2-y^2 can be factored into $(x+y)(x-y)$. But the expression of the physically real Pythagorean theorem's x^2+y^2 can only be factored algebraically as $(x+iy)(x-iy)$. Similarly Gauss showed that prime numbers, the seeming bedrock of all counting numbers, are dependent on impossible numbers, as for example, in the case of all $4n+1$ that are primes, such as 5. Such numbers are not really prime, as they can be factored, such as $5=(2+i)(2-i)$.

completing the formal rules of arithmetic, but rather by the physical process of direction which, he emphasized in contradistinction to Kant, could not be derived by "pure reason."[3] In his own doctoral dissertation on the fundamental theorem of algebra, Gauss had demonstrated this, which had caused quite a stir when it was issued. But even though his notebooks were filled with many developments on the subject of what had become known as complex numbers, his published work on the subject was almost nothing.

Into this environment came Riemann, who sought out Gauss as a doctoral advisor. In 1851, Gauss supervised Riemann's revolutionary dissertation on "Functions of a Complex Variable." Though the work is most often falsely relegated to the domain of pure mathematics, anyone who has studied Gauss and Riemann knows that that is not true. In fact, in his dissertation and his other works on Abelian Functions and Hypergeometric Functions, Riemann laid down a method of physical thinking that uncovered the connection between the way the mind works, and the physical universe works, and that it was only by gaining a deeper understanding of the former, that science could hope to grasp anything meaningful about the latter.

The core of Riemann's thinking is rooted in Leibniz's ideas of *least action* and *analysis situs*. Leibniz had insisted, in opposition to Descartes and the pragmatists of his time, that nothing irrational could happen in the universe, as that would render the human mind irrelevant. Consequently, the universe must be governed by principles that were not directly observable by the senses, but were nevertheless knowable by the human mind. One such concept is the principle of least action.

This is best illustrated pedagogically by an example. When light strikes a mirror, it is reflected at the same angle that it strikes the mirror (**Figure 1**). This is an observation verifiable in the domain of sense perception. But sense perception is incapable of answering the question, why does light act in this way? The formulation of the question, and its answer, is an act of mind acting in and on the universe. Ancient scientists had al-

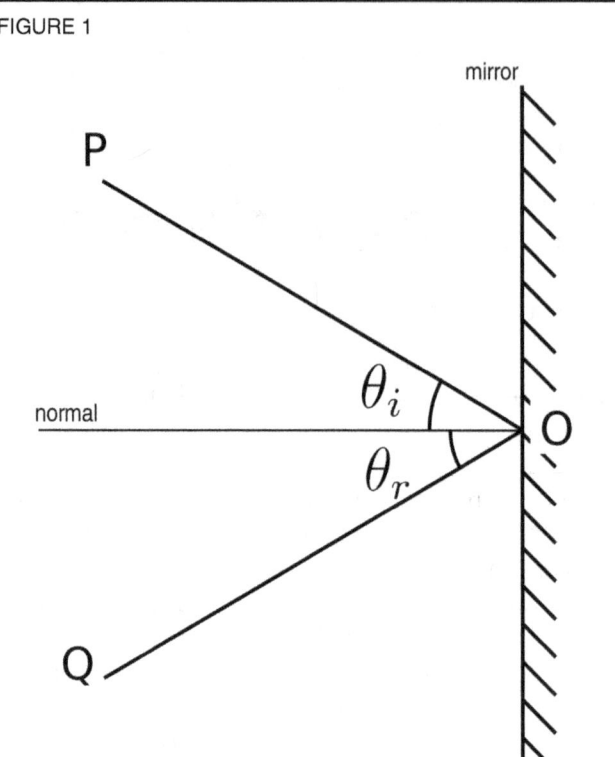

3. See Gauss' "Second Treatise on Biquadratic Residues" cited by Riemann in his habilitation dissertation. Gauss noted that the notion of positive and negative numbers indicated magnitudes situated in opposite directions, and that "imaginary" numbers indicated magnitudes orthogonal to the "real" numbers. He hypothesized the existence of a third set of numbers orthogonal to the real and imaginary, but never developed the idea. Riemann showed that this was unnecessary.

FIGURE 1

ready recognized that the equality of the angle of incidence with the angle of reflection meant that the overall path of the light was the shortest possible distance. Is this a particular characteristic of light, or only a special case applicable to this particular phenomenon?

When light travels through two different media, such as air and water, the angle of incidence and the angle of refraction are not equal[4] and, consequently, the path of the light is no longer the shortest distance (**Figure 2**). Is this a violation of the principle observed in the case of reflection?

Pierre de Fermat (1601-65) showed that the behavior of light under refraction, did not actually violate the principle of shortest path observed in reflection, but, rather, it reflected a higher concept of "path." Since the light changed its speed between the media, the shortest path had to be understood as the path of *least time*.

Leibniz saw this behavior of light as a reflection of a more universal concept that he called the "principle of least action," which, he emphasized, reflected the functional congruence of the creative powers of the human mind with the organization of the universe itself.

4. Though the angles of incidence and refraction are not equal, the sines of these angles are in constant proportion.

FIGURE 2

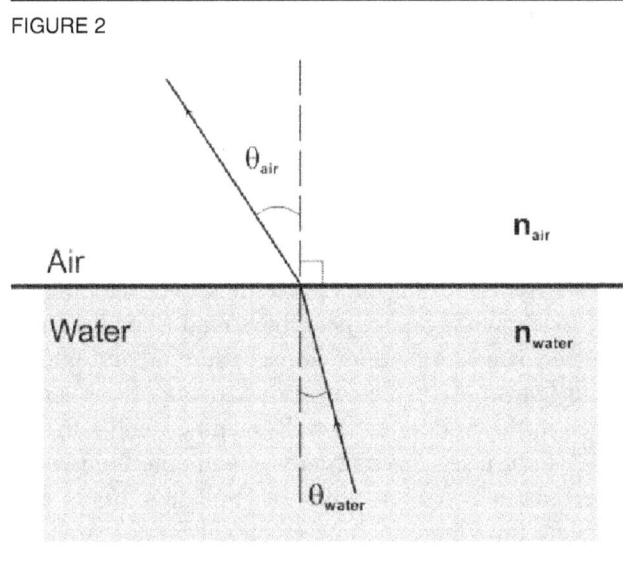

$$n_{air} < n_{water}$$

From this foundation, Riemann created an entirely new way of thinking. He conceived of the idea that the investigation of physics must be centered, not on the phenomena, but on physical manifolds. Over the course of many works, Riemann developed the notion of a physical manifold as a single conception under which a multiplicity of physical principles act. It is the nature of the manifold, accessible to the mind, but not sense perception, that determines the phenomena under investigation. Hence, abstract geometries and formal mathematical structures are discarded as useless.

Physical Manifolds

For example, from Riemann's standpoint, the difference between the behavior of reflected and refracted light, is not an effect of two different phenomena, but the same phenomenon acting in manifolds of different degrees of action. Reflection takes place in a manifold in which only direction changes, whereas refraction occurs in a manifold in which both direction and speed change.[5] What didn't change is the governing principle of least action. The expression of least action is, thus, conceived as a function of the characteristics of the manifold.

Riemann discovered that the domain of the complex numbers, having their origin in the interaction between the mind and nature, was uniquely suited to express the essential characteristics of a physical manifold. He called the principle at work here the "Dirichlet"[6] principle, which said that any bounded manifold expressed the principle of least action in a unique way. Riemann realized that this is expressed by a system of curves of minimum and maximum curvature which were always orthogonal to each other.[7] Because orthogonality is a physical expression of complex numbers, functions of a complex variable are uniquely suited to express the least action principle in physical manifolds.

This became the basis for Riemann to develop a general theory of manifolds in which he showed that only a small number of parameters, specifically the boundary conditions and number of singularities, determined the characteristic paths of least action.

Riemann went still further. The scientist, like the statesman or military leader, must discover the characteristics of a manifold as an active participant in the action. Friedrich Schiller described this in terms of creating political freedom as akin to fixing the mechanism of a clock while the clock is still running. This requires being able to discern the global characteristics of a manifold from its infinitesimal action.

Such an approach was not new to Riemann. Johannes Kepler had accomplished his results by determining the general characteristics of the solar system from a moving planet within it, by recognizing changes in the infinitesimally small. Thus every small part of a planet's motion reflected the overall characteristics of what Kepler understood as the solar system as a whole. We now know that the effects of galactic and intergalactic processes are also at work here. This was recognized by Riemann who, in his habilitation dissertation, emphasized that science must look into the very large and very small to understand nature.

Kepler's approach was further developed into the infinitesimal calculus by Leibniz, who formulated a more general approach that he called *analysis situs.* Gauss, in his investigations into geodesy and terrestrial magnetism, extended Leibniz's method, showing that such global characteristics as curvature and shortest

---

5. The former being a manifold of space, while the latter is a manifold of space-time.

6. Named for Lejeune Dirichlet, his predecessor at Göttingen. Dirichlet had been a protégé of Gauss and Alexander von Humboldt. Riemann had studied with Dirichlet for a year in Berlin. As the husband of Rebecca Mendelssohn, Dirichlet was involved in organizing collaboration among musicians and scientists when he came to Göttingen. Riemann participated in these collaborations.

7. Riemann's work here is a generalization of Gauss's concept of potential.

path (geodetic) could be determined from infinitesimally small measurements. For example, Gauss was the first person to determine the characteristics of the Earth's magnetic field, and the location of the south magnetic pole, purely from a careful *analysis situs* of small local variations in the Earth's magnetic field.

But Riemann took this even further. Elaborating a theory of functions of a complex variable, Riemann created a means by which the essential physical characteristics of a general manifold could be known from very small measurements, thus restoring the primacy of concepts over calculations in science. For anyone wishing to provide leadership in the domain of politics or economics today, a thorough grasp of Riemann's method is essential.

The elaboration of Riemann's theory of complex functions gives us a sense of Riemann's conceptual approach. But he was not a mere theorist. Riemann applied this method to some of the most outstanding problems in physics of his time, in the fields of electromagnetism, hydrodynamics, and geodesy. His efforts in these areas of applied physics repeatedly led to discoveries that showed that the reductionist methods which were in widespread use at the time, were not only conceptually inferior, but also produced wrong results.

Physics and Life

One of the best examples is Riemann's work on what has become known as shock-waves. In a compressible medium such as air, sound waves appear as alternating regions of compression and decompression of the air. It is a well-known observation that such waves propagate at a finite speed that is independent of the frequency (perceived as pitch) or the amplitude (perceived as volume) of the wave. From the above description and the mathematical analysis of a wave function, it would appear that this finite speed of sound is a limiting velocity that can not be surpassed. Riemann, however, saw it completely differently. He realized that if the alternating regions of compression and decompression overtook each other, a new state of organization would come into existence, creating a new structure that would propagate through the air at its own speed as if it were itself a material object. Today such structures are commonly known as "shock-waves." Riemann's hypothesis concerning shock-waves was considered ludicrous by the experts at the time. After his death, the experimental demonstration of shock-waves proved him right and his detractors short-sighted.

Once again, Riemann showed that mind, not mathematical formalism, reflects the world.

Toward the end of his life, Riemann began to investigate his long-held conviction that progress in science could only take place if the boundary between abiotic physics and living organisms were superseded. In his last work, Riemann presented his research into the mechanism of the human hearing apparatus. Analyzed as an abiotic mechanism, as Hermann von Helmholtz had done, human beings perceive sound when the compression waves of the air impact the tympanic membrane (eardrum), which in turn activates three small bones in the middle ear (anvil, hammer, and stirrup), which in turn set into motion a wave in the fluid in the inner ear, which then vibrates small hair fibers that translate the vibrations into electrical impulses which are perceived by the brain as sound.

The above approach attempts to explain the action of a living organism as if it were a collection of abiotic physical machines. Riemann noted that this was patently absurd. Were Helmholtz's theory true, then human beings could not be able to perceive the very subtle variations in timbre, volume, pitch, and nuance that make possible the discernment of language and polyphonic music. Though Riemann died before he could further elaborate an approach to understanding hearing, his study posits the exciting and provocative idea that the investigation of all physical processes must be subsumed by the higher concept of life. In this way, Riemann laid the foundations for the breakthroughs in this direction by Vladimir Vernadsky, and set the stage for new areas of science that are yet to be explored.

This approach did not come late in life to Riemann. When his papers were compiled after his death, a series of fragments on mind, life, and philosophy were discovered that give us an insight into the source of his remarkable ability to see far beyond the appearances. These works, published posthumously as his Philosophical Fragments, show that all of Riemann's thinking about physics started with a deep appreciation of the creative powers of the mind. It is his concept of how the mind works that is reflected in his thinking on how the physical world functions.

It is best to let Riemann speak for himself:

With each simple act of thinking, something durable, substantial enters our mind. This substance appears to us, in fact, as a unity, but it appears (insofar as it is the expression of space and time extension) as comprising a subsumed manifold; I name this a *thought-mass*. To this effect, all thinking is the development of new thought-masses. The thought-masses entering into the mind appear to us to be images; their varying internal states determine how they differ qualitatively.

As they are forming, the thought-masses blend; or are folded together, or connect to one another and also to older thought-masses, in a precisely determined manner. The character and strength of these connections depend upon causes which were only partially recognized by Johann Friedrich Herbart, but which I shall fill out in what follows. They rest primarily on the internal relationships among the thought-masses.

The mind is a compact, multiply connected thought-mass with internal connections of the most intimate kind. It grows continuously as new thought-masses enter it, and this is the means by which it continues to develop. Thought-masses once formed, are imperishable; and their connections cannot be dissolved; only the relative strength of these connections is altered by the addition of new thought-masses.

Thought-masses need no material carrier for their continued existence, and exert no lasting effect upon the physical world. Therefore they are not related to any portion of matter, and have no position in space. On the other hand, a material carrier is required for every entry, generation, every formation of new thought-masses, and for their unification. Thus all thinking does occur at a definite place.

In other fragments, Riemann noted that this process of concept formation was inherently social, transmitted through culture and language within and across generations. He further indicated that the development of ideas in human beings is the highest expression of a universal process that encompasses the living and non-living domains.

For its continued survival, the human race desperately needs a revival of scientific thinking of the quality of Riemann. A first step would be to rediscover what Riemann actually did and thought, which is something of which almost no one alive today, except Lyndon LaRouche, has much of an understanding.

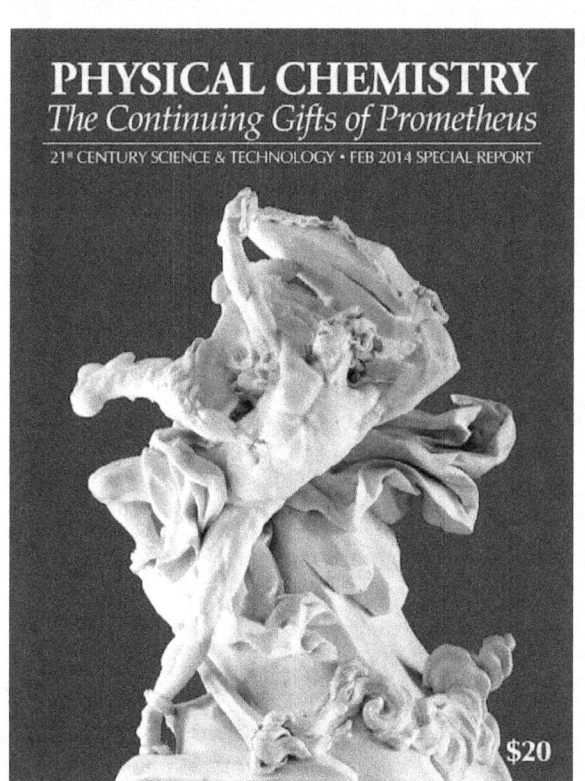

Editorial

Looking for His Glasses, Kicked in the Rear

From Lyndon LaRouche's Dialogue with the LaRouche PAC Policy Committee of April 25

Lyndon LaRouche: This is going to be a very interesting situation, for two reasons. One, is that the juveniles, so to speak, will assume that everything is easily laid down neatly for them, and the fact is that it is not. For example, there are radical changes going around, and it's not going to be fixed. It's going to be tough, and so forth. So that's crucial. People will say, "oh, this is what's going to happen. This is what's going to happen. This is what's going to happen." And none of it is true. And we just went through this weekend, on this thing, going through this, and there is nothing there that is going to be the same as people thought would be the same.

And so therefore, I think, for that reason, I think it's important that we put an emphasis of clarity on the fact that we cannot rely upon what the apparent conditions are like at any one time in this region. The thing is much too unstable. And therefore, when people would draw conclusions and say, "oh, so and so, now that's where it's going to be." And that is not where it's going to be.

And that's the kind of problem we have to consider ourselves, here, of things that bear on that kind of problem. Don't assume that there is something that you can draw a conclusion from. You can't. But the point is, that there is no specific position of motion, which can be located exactly.

I went into this thing on Sunday. And I can tell you that what Obama thinks he's got on his hands, is not what he has on his hands. That he is being moved into something by the British on the one hand, and by the others on the other hand. So this thing is not a fixed system. It's going to jump. It's going to be surprises. And you're going to find the person is looking for his glasses, and finds himself being kicked in the rear end.

No Fixed Geographies

Host Matthew Ogden: It's been a relentless two-week pile-on against Obama, in particular, around the cover-up of the 28 pages. And we could very well be seeing the fall of the House of Saud, if not the fall of the House of Windsor. And to the extent that Obama continues to declare his love for King Salman and Queen Elizabeth, you can see the fall of the House of Obama, as well, not to mention the fall of the House of Bush.

LaRouche: And it's all British. The whole thing is completely the British Empire. So the question is, we've got to destroy the British Empire. That's the first thing. So therefore, how do you do that? Well, that's a multiple effort, which means that what we have to look for, is when people think that, "well, this is what's going to happen," they are probably wrong, and that they don't understand how this thing works. They think in terms of fixed geographies, and they don't exist, not in this operation. Because, people can move around rather rapidly these days, and they will do that. Just like he, our friend [Putin], will do. He does tend to jump into new territories very quickly.

So, no, but the point is, the idea that there is a fixed map, of any sense of map, in the terms of what is happening now, in terms of the trans-Atlantic period, alone, that thing was not going to be stable. We'll know some specific things that could be available, or likely to be. So we have to have an open mind for understanding, and *don't* assume that you found gold. You didn't find the great gold mass. You just found something new. Or maybe it found you.

The point is, there's a principle involved here, not just a thing, but a principle. And the principle is that all kinds of things can happen, and jump from one place to another, or jump to combinations of places and others, or to sudden changes in the thing. So there is not. World

War II was for a bunch of pansies, compared to what we're facing from this kind of situation presently.

Benjamin Deniston of the Science Team: I mean one aspect that's hanging over the whole situation is the financial system. The whole trans-Atlantic financial system is bankrupt.

LaRouche: Yeah, the interesting thing though, that in all of this, there is nothing provided for progress in that kind of system. There is no progressive system [in those] games. And that's what the interest is. And we can get more into that. But it's really fun. It's really fun, because we find, *we're going beyond Earth*. That is, we're going beyond Earth, as we've understood it. And what's going to happen, the people who are playing things, smart people, are going to jump away from what they call the usual systems. Because they will react to the expansion, of play, which is provided in space. In space and the future of mankind will lie chiefly in what happens *in space*.

Part of the key problems is that the typical American, or the typical of most nations, has no understanding whatsoever, of how actually the human species is now in the process of moving toward *changes* in its characteristic behaviors, which they have never seen before. And it will happen inherently. Because you have a broader area in which to operate, and what Kesha's doing in Texas, there, that operation, and what she's got is a little nest building up there, for organization purposes; and this is going to *change everything*. And so all the fixed notions, the fixed positions, are going to *vanish*. Why will they vanish? Because we need more room for the real things.

Kesha Rogers of Houston: Yeah, it's true, that the Chinese right now, they're actually taking up the space program from this conception of what is the prerogative of mankind? What is the destiny of mankind? What should be the defining purpose of mankind in the Solar System? And I thought it was very exciting yesterday, that China announced for the first time, a National Space Day, which was yesterday, April 24th. They had educators, scientists, teachers teaching young people, students, and so-forth, about the mission of the Chinese space program, their commitment to landing on far side of the Moon, building a corridor of development to the Moon, and to the planets beyond, and so forth.

And you asked, what is the American intention to bring about such an initiative, such a national mission?

And, it's not there.

But we could actually be doing something to really not allow for these people's work, and their contributions to be in vain. And the idea about that, is not just to recognize a certain day, or a person who went into space, and who contributed to the mission, but more so, to recognize that this is human destiny. This is our prerogative. And it's a higher conception in terms of what we have to do to build peaceful relations among nations, and to break with this insane geopolitics.

No Fixed Positions

LaRouche: Oh, I got an experience of that during 1971, because we were going through all kinds of changes at that time. I got involved in kicking the British system out of existence for a while. And they said, "You got us this time, but we're going to get you next time!" kind of thing, and so the operation I was running as the interim operation which I was assigned to, and this all worked. But what that means is, that what happens is, everything you think you have fixed, *is probably not fixed*. The lesson that people have to learn, very quickly.

Rachel Brinkley of Boston: What we have now, I think, which is fixed in a certain way, is the principle of New York as a quality of the future, and the modern city on the hill. It used to be Boston, and that didn't work; now New York is really the city on the hill for the United States, the place that is calling for freedom, for true freedom for mankind. And I think what we're seeing with this 9/11 quality is that: It's a principle of justice, of ending the tyranny that has taken the lives of our citizens—both those who were murdered and those who were not murdered. So Manhattan can lead us to the future.

LaRouche: Yes!

Diane Sare of Manhattan: On that, I'll just say, it is the case, there is a different kind of dynamic in New York, as this material begins to come out on the Saudi role, and it becomes public. Because people are angry. The population there was very profoundly affected by the events of 9/11, and the people you meet will tell you where they were, that day, when it happened; what happened to them. One woman we just met remembers trying to get on the subway out of lower Manhattan and what was going on there. And they are not backing off it.

And there was a run yesterday, a memorial for 9/11, I think organized by the museum. It was completely sold out in terms of the runners who were allowed, maybe 1,000 or so; and then a few thousand other family members came. We were there with our leaflets on the role of the Queen, the Saudis and Obama, and people were not flinching. People are furious at Obama. There was *no* defense of him; no defense of his role in this. This is a *shift*.

LaRouche: Yes. It's a shift, it has implications which go way beyond what people would think is the consequence.

Ogden: I think what's important to note on that, is people have referenced the role of Congressman Walter Jones as being one of the initial catalysts in this bill to declassify the 28 pages, H.Res.14, formerly H.Res.428. But why was he able to conceive of the fact, that there was a massive lie coming from the Bush administration, around the facts of the matter on 9/11? Because *he* was lied to directly by Dick Cheney, around the weapons of mass destruction in Iraq! He *knew, personally,* — sitting where we are, across the table —

LaRouche: When you look at the Bush family, look at its history. Remember there was a continuous degeneration by the Bush family, in moving from one war to another. And the other war was what we just recently experienced.

Therefore, the question is, we cannot operate on the basis of a fixed conception. We have to operate on the basis of what is *not* a fixed position, but rather something which is giving you a change. And this is something which most people in the United States, and Europe also, have no conception of what that kind of thing means. They have no understanding, they're absolutely incompetent in this kind of matter, because they don't realize that the most important developments in history have been actions which started as one thing, and then turned out to be something quite different, as a decisive action. And that is what most people in the United States today *have no comprehension of this at all.* And this is why people kill themselves, by poisoning themselves, and so forth.

Because they've lost all connection to the future. And they're frightened. They're afraid that some mysterious force is going to grab them, and kill them. But these are the kinds of conditions we're facing, is new ones, because the idea that babies were born, and they grew up, and people became new babies, like the old, or something like the old. And people say, "well, that's the way it is, we're stuck!" We're fixed in a situation, where we have to conform to a kind of behavior, just like Bush, young Bush. The same kind of thing. And therefore, you get a period of a sense of destitution entirely, because they don't know what the next step is. They don't know that a new step is coming. And they're surprised.

This is exactly what happened, with the SDI operation, that we with. It was that, we changed everything. We had a good team, and we did it. But then, what happened, once the Bush family got its claws into this thing, and Reagan was neutralized, that that's how the whole process that has happened, did happen.

A Much Bigger Question

Bill Roberts of Detroit: I saw something recently where there's a problem with a lot of the people who survived 9/11 that they've lived with what's called "survivors' guilt," and it has gripped them, this entire time of the last 10, 15 years, that "why did I survive, and these other people died?" as if the only way to resolve this, is, "how do I dedicate myself to actually making these people's lives being lost, where there's something that's resolved about this?" And I think that this question has to actually be brought up, to change the entire international situation. Because I think that is what looms over this entire thing: It's a much bigger question than just the Saudis and 9/11. The United States has been used as part of a function of an empire, and people have to actually face that, to actually resolve this issue of what 9/11 was.

LaRouche: Well, your argument really has probably more importance than you yourself might suspect.

The point is, if mankind is able to step out of a role, which is like some practical way of working, or things like that, and if mankind can do that, then mankind is actually becoming a superior development with respect to human beings generally. In other words, if you can take a human being, or a group of human beings, or category of human beings, and you find that these people will develop as something which they had not developed originally; and therefore, they will go in a new direction and develop a new theory and a new intention, and this is what will move them in that new direction.

And therefore, the obvious thing is if you want to educate the population of the planet, that's the way you have to look at it. You have to say, "You cannot tell these kiddos that they're going to do this for the rest of their life. You cannot do that!" I don't care how smart you are, you cannot be allowed to do that! Therefore, you have to realize you have to search, always, for opportunities which exist *beyond*, what you have known heretofore. Once you grab onto that, then you'll find kiddies will start grabbing around each other, and saying "let's play with these toys." And they should come up with new discoveries — and that's what *did* happen, in the new discoveries, that's exactly what happened.

So actually, it was not something that the child had built into them, but it's something where the child was *changed* from what they had been! Changed because of the necessity for going to a higher level of achievement, in order to escape the limitations of the past.

Deniston: You're talking about the very essence that defines mankind as something different that other forms of life we see. The characteristic of mankind in the most basic sense, is that we can fundamentally, willfully intervene, to self-change our relationship to the Universe. We can create a new state of existence for our species, in a way that's unique, completely unique. And there's something unique about the human mind and human culture that enables mankind uniquely to do that.

LaRouche: That was exactly what my intention was when I did this thing on going to the Moon. Because that's exactly it: You have to find — it's absolutely necessary, you can't escape it; you cannot live within some kind of an object that you hold in your hands like a toy, to play with. What you have to do is find something which is important, which has a clear importance built into it, and you have the ability to understand, to *create something new*, which goes beyond the bounds of what people had heretofore believed were the limits for their existence.

Can you create in yourself, something which you had never been able to do, independently. And you find that you grab on something like that, and say *"This* is the thing that's going to make the next step for mankind better!"

Deniston: But I think your opening point about not assuming anything, at this point I think is a very wise and appropriate message to put up front.

LaRouche: It's something that has to happen, because if you can't do that, you lose the ability to create.

www.ingramcontent.com/pod-product-compliance
Lightning Source LLC
Chambersburg PA
CBHW081156280526
45787CB00008B/3357